A Ringer's Hands

A Ringer's Hands

Andy Hughes

Copyright © 2012 Andy Hughes

This book is copyright. Apart from any fair dealing for the purpose of private study, research, criticism or review, as permitted under the Copyright Act, no part may be reproduced by any process without written permission. Enquiries should be addressed to the Publishers.

All rights reserved.

First published 2012

National Library of Australia Cataloguing-in-Publication entry:

Author:	Hughes, Andy.
Title:	A ringer's hands / Andy Hughes.
ISBN:	9781921920448 (pbk.)
	9781921920455 (ebook)
Subjects:	Hughes, Andy.
	Stockmen--Northern Territory--Biography.
	Ranchers--Northern Territory--Biography.
	Northern Territory--Social life and customs.
	Murranji Station (N.T.).
Dewey Number:	626.201092

Typeset in Perpetua 12pt.

Cover Design: Boolarong Press

Published by Boolarong Press, Salisbury, Brisbane, Australia.

Printed and bound by Watson Ferguson & Company, Salisbury, Brisbane, Australia.

For my family and friends

Please enjoy

A special thanks to my mate Darrell Lewis

Contents

'It was pleasant up the country, City Bushman, where you went, for you sought the greener patches and you travelled like a gent.'

The City Bushman,
Henry Lawson 1892

Preface

My grandfather's favourite book was *We of the Never Never*. He'd read long passages in a deep and passionate voice to a captivated ten year old, hanging on every word. 'Houselessness is not necessarily homelessness,' he'd say, and talk romantically of the 'scrub and open plains that make the backbone of Australia,' and the resourceful men and women that built families and working properties 'out there.' The stories of his time jackarooing in a remote part of South Australia are lost, and the long tales of riding station horses, living in stock camps and working cattle are gone with him, but the spirit lives on in the memories of his listeners.

Sydney was never quite right for me. It offered everything I needed to survive and strive but it offered none of the romance that my grandfather spoke of. I always knew I'd never be completely whole until I went on a muster, or slept in a swag in a drover's camp – a lot of young people in the city could really benefit from such things. A year working in the outback goes by so quickly that it seems over before it's begun, but the experiences live forever – please enjoy some of mine here.

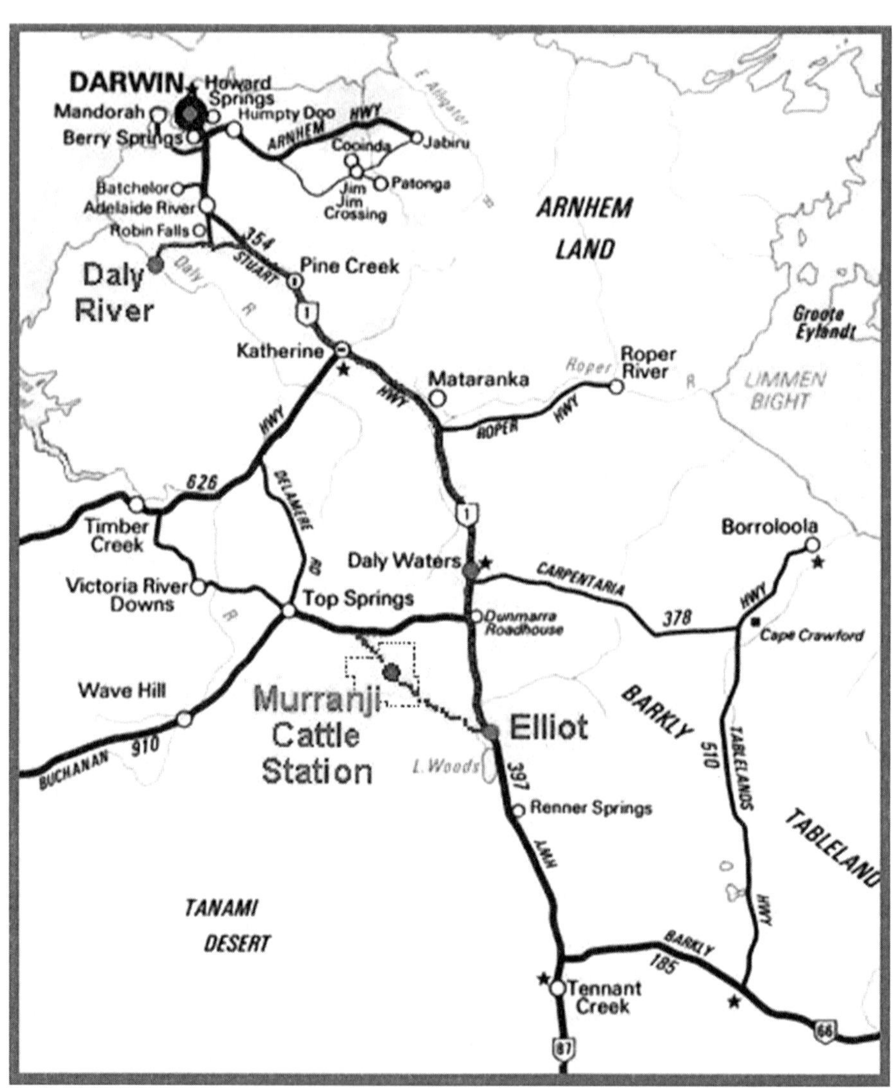

Map of the Northern Territory showing Murranji cattle station (outlined in middle), Elliot (closest township) and Daly Waters (site of the famous rodeo).

Introduction

Murranji Cattle Station is located in the middle of the Northern Territory – the 'Top End' of Australia. In 1987 when I arrived at Murranji, the station was nearly five thousand square kilometres, bigger than the Sydney metropolitan area. The northern boundary was the Buchanan Highway in the north and to the south and west was the Tanami Desert. The eastern boundary was sixty miles from the homestead, at the edge of Newcastle Waters Station.

Murranji straddles the famous Murranji Track which traverses some of Australia's harshest country, dense with the spiny branches of bullwaddy scrub and endless stretches of lancewood forest. The Track extends from the historic homestead of Newcastle Waters to Top Springs, 225kms to the northwest and in its day it was known as one of the toughest stock routes in the country. For the better part of the twentieth century it was an important shortcut for droving teams pushing mobs of cattle out of the Kimberley region in the far north and across the Barkly Tableland to Queensland in the southeast. For the latter part of the century it was a tough section of the Round Australia Rally, or 'Redex Trials.'

During the two-month wet season, around Christmas each year, intense tropical storms roll across Murranji from the north, dumping life-giving rain on parched ground. The dust turns to mud, and after a couple of weeks the plains turn green with the new growth of long spindly grasses and tall stands of pea-bush. Around mid-March the rains stop, and the ground begins to dry out and turn hard again. The pea-bush turns brittle and the grasses change to brown. Creeks stop flowing and the small number of scattered waterholes evaporate quickly.

For most of the year it's hard country. Water is hard to find, the days are hot and the nights can get very cold. Only tough cattle survive up there, and Brahman are the toughest. They grow fat and healthy on the hardy grasses that endure the extreme changes from wet season to dry.

Some of the better-looking young bulls were held back, but most were 'cut' – lost their manhood to a ringer's knife. These grew into big steers and were then sent off on crowded road trains to abattoirs in Katherine for the domestic market, or up to Darwin to be loaded onto special boats to feed the international livestock trade to end up packed in clear plastic and styrofoam for hungry shoppers.

Murranji had a holding capacity of between two and four head per square kilometre, which meant that on most years the station could run more than ten thousand head. Among them there was always a small number of 'cleanskins' – a heifer or bull that has grown up never coming into contact with a human, an animal that has never been mustered, caught, or branded.

Murranji Cattle Station, Northern Territory, from the air, looking towards the northwest. You can see open black soil plains in the foreground, dry sand and desert at the top and bullwaddy scrub stretching out to the west.

'Apart from extremely short-lived waters that appear immediately after rainfall — shallow claypans or gilgais — there are very few surface waters on the Murranji and none of them are permanent. For six to eight months of the year the Murranji is virtually waterless, and during this time it constitutes an arid forest.'

The Murranji Track, Ghost Road of the Drovers,
Darrell Lewis

CHAPTER 1
DRIVING ON

Northern Territory, Murranji Cattle Station, March 1987

'Hold his head up or his eyes'll fall out!' The Head Stockman yelled.

It was my first day on the cattle station — one I'll never likely forget. I'd been driving all day but was finally there. A day earlier I'd run into an old mate in Katherine who told me about seasonal work on offer at Murranji — a property south of Katherine near the little town of Elliott. 'Go south on the Stuart Highway for about 400 kilometres to a roadhouse called Dunmara. After that, turn right at the second cattle grid and follow that track, no matter what. Drive for about two hours and you'll see the homestead on a small hill.'

I organised a full tank of petrol, bought a fresh packet of tobacco and headed south. Turning at the second cattle grid as instructed, I found myself on a dusty track heading west. Saltbush and crusty clay-pan stretched out for miles in front, and far off in the distance a treeline stretched across the horizon. Following the track, over wide flat plains and through long stretches of thick scrub, I passed small mobs of hardy-looking cattle and the odd wallaby looking on absently from a safe distance as I drove on. Then three camels loped across the track and I thought I'd driven clear out of the country! Finally, way out in the distance a cluster of houses appeared, the quarters and sheds that was the homestead complex which would be my home for the next ten months — Murranji Cattle Station.

'Don't ride him long sunshine. Tuck him in or you'll go over!'

The hollering was coming from the main yards, a sprawling steel affair that looked as though it was built to hold wild buffalo. And at times that was nearly what did go through those sturdy looking gates and fences. A couple of blokes were working an angry horse in the midday sun.

'Give it to him Garry, don't take no shit!'

I pulled up in my old Valiant ute about twenty yards from the scene of all the excitement and crossed the distance at a steady walk, not wanting to look eager or trip over my boots. I'd done a bit of horse riding when I was growing up, trail rides here and there, a bit on a big bay lad that belonged to a friend in Sydney, and on a buckskin on a small place north-west of the city. My seat was okay and I liked to pretend I could be a 'lonestar cowboy' like the gunslingers who raced around on big black horses in Sunday afternoon TV westerns. But I'd never seen what I was about to witness that first day on Murranji.

'That's it Garry, you've got him now.'

A wiry little blackfella was astride a lathered roan horse that was trying its best to kill itself and everyone else in sight. The black skin of his arms glistened with sweat as he was thrown around in the saddle. A whitefella with a dusty black hat was standing in the middle of the yard with one hand on his belt buckle and the other held just off to the side, as if he was directing traffic. There were a couple of other ringers sitting on the top rails eagerly watching the action, and one was looking down on the action from what looked like the backseat of an old VW welded to the top rail.

The horse bucked and pig-rooted, heaved, and breathed heavily. The rider was tossed around like a rag doll but somehow managed to stay in the saddle. He looked loose and rubbery and his legs were straight, then bent, then straight again. He held his left arm way out to the back to give himself leverage and balance, and his right arm held the reins loosely out in front. Even with my limited experience I could tell the big horse was nearly done. The rider was positively disappointed when the roan gave up its fight and slowed to a steady lope around the boundary of the breaking yard.

'Good job Garry, you done him.' Then, 'Look Out!'

Yells and falling bodies were the sudden result of the steed's final protest. As horse and rider loped past the men sitting on the steel fence the horse made a double-barreled attempt to kill them all. I was taken aback by the power so suddenly unleashed by the back end of the angry horse. It took a few minutes for things to settle down again, and a few more before someone decided to acknowledge the presence of the tall white boy standing near the yards.

'Bet you've never seen riding like that before hey city boy?'

Garry Stephens, the rider of the big roan and the man responsible for picking my background straight away, was the one who spoke. What was it that gave me away? The ute was covered in a fine layer of road grime from many miles of highway, and you could hardly see the spotlights mounted on the bull bar through a thick layer of dead insects. I hadn't spoken or even gestured in any way. I'd been travelling for three months and five thousand kilometres, driving up the east coast from Sydney all the way to Cairns, and then across Queensland and into the Territory. Living hard and frugal, I'd camped in heat and cold and packed up in rain. I had a well-worn Akubra hat and an easy-going slouch, and I thought I'd washed the city completely off by the time I'd reached the Top End.

Over the next ten months I witnessed some of the most breathtakingly beautiful scenes that nature could conjure up. I discovered my limits of physical endurance and pain, and then those limits were tested. I saw humanity and inhumanity, rough acts by hard men on weaker men and unfortunate animals. Blood was spilt. And I developed many bonds with horses and with people, men who had seen rough times, a lot of rough country miles and a lot of satisfying good times. Men who became work mates who would watch my back, and me theirs. The Territory is tough country requiring a tough attitude. Outback stations are no place for the faint-hearted, but I'd been preparing for this moment for a long time.

No two days were alike at Murranji. On a Monday, if I bothered to check what day of the week it was on the girlie calendar on the wall as I rushed out the kitchen door, we could be riding out to one of the local mobs of cattle to push them back to the main yards for drafting. By Wednesday I might be driving out to a far-off bore with a ute-load of tools, a roll of fencing wire and a drum full of diesel to refill one of the precious life-giving water pumps. Over the course of the season I learned how to weld, to service a tractor, change a truck tyre, pull an engine apart and fix the leather of a saddle. I learnt basic plumbing, building, welding and electrical skills. I realised what my grandfather used to say held true: 'Being good with your hands is the mark of a man' and, 'There's a knack to everything. Find that knack and you're set.'

The value of a Northern Territory ringer is a unique measure. Respect is earned based on your ability with rope and leather on cattle and horse, not your background, history or name. Inquiries are not made into your level of schooling or whether or not you have a criminal record. And a lot of ringers have past lives better left alone. Women, ex-friends, bankers and quite a few policemen in southern states would be happy to find a certain ringer or two, but that doesn't matter up there. You work, you eat and you sleep, and the boss is always happiest when you confine your activities to those three basic things.

I was rudely woken most mornings before 5 o'clock and as the sun was coming up I'd be shuffling around the yards with up to a dozen other riders, saddling my horse for the day and getting ready to ride many kilometres before dinner. Some days were better than others, but most were full of laughter and action. As I gained experience I began to understand how it was that bets were made, stories told and songs written. I gambled poorly, had no story to tell, and couldn't sing to save myself — but I was ready to try.

"Hely Hutchinson who traversed the track in 1905 claimed that, "The dry stage between Newcastle River and Yellow Waterholes is dotted with little brown mounds, sad witness to the awful fate that overtook the poor fellows whose mortal clay occupies them.'

'Out Where the Dead Men Lie' The Murranji Track, Ghost Road of the Drovers,
Darrell Lewis

CHAPTER 2
City Boy

The horse-breakers told me to drive past the workshop, follow the track up to the homestead — the big house — and find the boss, Robert. I got back in my ute and drove towards the compound as instructed. My old mate in Katherine had told me the blokes at Murranji were 'better than the average bad bunch,' and he told me stories of jackaroos who had worked for months on other outback stations only to be sacked after three months, with an unsigned cheque and no options. One station boss in Halls Creek had taken to a couple of jackaroos with a shifting spanner and sent them walking down the long track back to town, just because they were sick and couldn't work that day. I hoped Murranji was different and desperately wanted to stay on for the whole season, to get stuck right in.

I drove around the workshop and across to the main house, parked the ute between a dusty police Toyota troop-carrier and an old blue Toyota tray-back, and looked around. The small group of buildings and sheds — the boss's house, the workshop, the head stockman's house and the workmen's quarters — was arranged in a rough square and set on a small hill surrounded by many kilometres of dusty red plains and long stretches of thick scrub. The small patches of manicured lawn in front of the main house and the workmen's quarters stood out as fluorescent bright green against the greys, browns and reds of the soil and scrub. The two most imposing structures in the compound were the water tank stand and the workshop. The water tank could've provided enough drinking water for a small country, and the workshop could easily have housed a plane the size of the legendary Spruce Goose.

A dust-covered tractor with a huge floor jack holding its rear end high in the air, and one of its wheels was lying next to it on the oil-stained concrete was parked just inside one of the workshop bays. A flatbed truck with its cab tilted forward and greasy handprints all over its mudguards was parked backwards in another bay. On a flat piece of ground about two hundred metres to the north I could make out four white cones which were markers for the start of the airstrip, and across the compound there was a little shed with wide eaves and flyscreen walls which I guessed must have been the meat-house. Young spindly trees were planted at random around the compound, with timber pallets stacked on their sides to act as temporary protection from hungry animals. As I stood there taking it all in I could hear the faint sounds of the men yelling at each other down at the yards, and every now and then the clang of a steel gate slamming shut.

I walked through the creaky little iron gate at the head of the path and headed towards the front door. Along the veranda stood neat rows of tall shiny black riding boots, dusty brown work boots, and a pair of old blue thongs. A pair of gumboots with dry, cracked mud on the outside and what looked like a wasps' nest on the inside lay abandoned under a deck chair. There were strange tools, horse rigging and unrecognisable bits of steel and leather hanging up along the wall, and above my head along the edge of the veranda roof was a long row of cow's heads in varying degrees of decomposition. As I approached the front door the sound of low voices came from the front room so stepping up to the screen door I knocked, and stood back a pace.

From inside I heard the quick scurrying of small feet and the slower, heavier sound of large boots. The door was flung wide and I found myself looking down at a very dainty Asian lady who bowed slightly and said, with a thick accent, 'Hello young man, can I help you?'

'I've come about a jackaroo job. I've heard you're looking for crew?' I said in reply.

A shadow fell over the lady at the door as the boss stepped out from the side room into the doorway and produced a dinner plate-sized hand for shaking. I strained to keep a relaxed smile on my face as the meat was squeezed out of my soft right hand. 'Great!' he said, and called back over his shoulder, 'Come on men, we've found our driver!'

He pushed past me and moved out onto the veranda as two khaki-clad policemen and two black trackers came out of a side room where they'd been discussing their current problem. They shoved rough hands at me to say hello and introduce themselves. I grit my teeth through the repeated pain. Then they walked me down the pathway, out the iron gate and over to the old blue Toyota. They were talking about some mission they were about to embark upon which made no sense to me. Something about 'tracking out to the Tanami' and something else about 'awful business' and 'women trouble.'

'My name's Rob. I'm the Manager here,' said the boss as he walked up to where I was standing beside the two trackers. 'Welcome to Murranji, you start straight away.'

'Thanks' I said, and introduced myself as 'Andy, from down south.'

'Well, Andy from down south,' said Rob, 'Get ready for some months of cattle, campfires and calluses.'

Rob explained they were going to drive southwest from the homestead to bring back a bloke who had walked off towards the desert. 'The trackers here will tell you which way to go,' he said as he walked away towards the other vehicle, 'We'll follow in the police truck.' I was quick to learn that whatever Rob said, you did. Not just because he was the boss, or because he was twice your size, or because he'd lived in the area his whole life and knew everything there was to know about station life, but simply because it could save my young life.

Jumping into the driver's seat as the two trackers climbed up onto the back, I started the engine and put the Tojo into gear as though this was just another day on the farm. From the passenger-side window of the police jeep Rob called to one of the trackers, 'Pick up his trail Pat. I want him back by sunset.' Then to me he said, 'Okay city boy, let's go.'

'City boy?' I wondered for the second time that day what it was that gave me away.

The next eight hours were about as bizarre as you can get. With minimal directions from the two men on the back of the Tojo (the name given to the common Toyota tray-back four wheel drive you see everywhere up there) we drove for two hours through some of the most incredible country that I'd ever seen. Through dense scrub, long stands of spiny, twisted bush and dense ti-tree, and over open plains of black soil where huge cracks criss-crossed the surface making the drive slow and bumpy.

Now and then a lone wallaby loped slowly along or from a safe distance stood to attention and watched the trucks pass. Further on we passed through stretches of red clay ground and over well-worn cattle tracks in limestone shale country. Occasionally the trackers on the back pounded on the roof and yelled at me to stop, and they got off to have a closer look at the ground ahead of the vehicle. Every so often we stopped at a fence line and one of the trackers jumped off the back and swung open a Queensland gate to let the small convoy through to the next big paddock. The further we went the more difficult it became to follow the track, and sometimes what looked like a track was really only a cattle pad.

'Look out for that bulldust! Shit, too late!'

'Bull-what?' At that moment I didn't know what all the yelling was for, and I had no idea what bulldust was. I was about to learn all about it.

The driver's-side front wheel crashed into a foot-deep hole filled to its brim with the finest black powdery dust, and the Tojo was launched into low-earth orbit. Luckily the truck came back down on all four wheels, closely followed by me from my perch near the ceiling of the cab. A great cloud of dust surrounded the vehicle, and when it cleared I looked through the back window to see if I still had my payload of one spare wheel, a toolbox, some fencing wire and two trackers. To my dismay all I had were the humans. The rest was scattered in random order across the paddock to the south.

I reversed and the three of us set about reloading as Rob and the cops turned up to warn me about the perils of driving through bulldust. That was my first lesson on Murranji, my first lesson in outback living. It was not so much about the bulldust but about the provision of information. The bloke who knows the danger in a situation, the bloke who can fill you in on the best, safest, quickest way of doing things, will ninety nine-times out of a hundred explain the process in great detail, with colourful additions and exaggerations and personal self-taught experience, AFTER you've gone through a life-threatening situation and nearly hospitalised yourself.

'Now you know what to watch out for?' asked one of the trackers, as he put his dusty Akubra back on his curly-haired head. 'We watch for sign, you watch for bulldust and holes.'

Thirty minutes later Pat leant in through the passenger-side window and said, 'Pull up over near that old windmill stand,' and I craned around to spot the landmark. 'That's Number Six Bore, he must've gone that way,' he said.

The boss, the two cops and the rest of us milled around the bore looking for sign. I watched the trackers as they circled the bore and talked to Rob. 'He was here only a couple of hours ago boss, the silly whitefella has walked most of this way with no shoes. He won't be far.'

Everyone got back into the vehicles and we drove on for another couple of kilometres. As we topped a small rise I had to squint to take a second look! Red sand-hills stretched out ahead of us as far as the eye could see. We'd reached the southern boundary of the property, the edge of the desolate and dangerous Tanami Desert. Until that moment I had no idea what the trackers were seeing in the rocky, dusty ground, but the tracks in the sand I was looking at right then were unmistakably human.

Like a group from the movie, Lawrence of Arabia, everyone followed the tracks over the low dunes, and it didn't take long before we found the man, stripped down to the waist and sitting cross-legged on the hot sand with his head lolling on his chest. I stood back with the trackers as the others moved forward. Nobody said anything, and there was a momentary pause as the man realised he was not going to die that day. The two policemen helped the stranger to his feet and they half-carried him back towards the vehicles. After a moment the rest of us followed. The landscape was suddenly surreal, like the set of some B-Grade Hollywood western, and as we walked into a fake sunset I thought a movie director was going to yell 'CUT, that's a wrap.' I was going to feel like that a lot over the coming months.

The trackers were travelling up front in the cabin with me as we headed back to the homestead. The return trip was a lot quieter than the trip out, and as we drove I wondered, 'What makes a man want to check out? How bad do things have to get?' With so much ahead, so much to do and learn and experience, I couldn't fathom what it took to make someone go that far. As it turned out, the bloke had been through a lot of grief. He'd had a wife and a little girl, but the wife had gone to live with another man who was now her husband, and had become the little girl's father. The poor bloke didn't want to think about it anymore. He was sick and tired of trying to survive and feed himself, and trying not to think about what could have been. His father had told him stories of the wonderful times he'd spent droving cattle through the outback as a jackaroo, before he met his mother and settled down to raise a family. He never went back to that life, but he used to tell his son about places in the scrub and the desert. Like me, the son was inspired to go outback, and when things went wrong for him the desert seemed like the perfect place to perish and decay, to get blown around on the wind.

Later, I realised what the strange expressions on the faces of the two policemen and the station manager meant that first day at Murranji. They were contemplating if they were actually doing the right thing. Should they be prolonging the inevitable for this man, or should they have not tried so hard to find him that day? Much later I realised I'd never asked the man's name.

Soon the policemen, the would-be suicide case, and the black trackers all went off down the track to town and I was left standing next to the boss in the fading evening light. After a while Rob pointed towards the workmen's quarters and said, 'You're first jackaroo here so far. That means you get the pick of the bunks. Fill the wood box and take really short showers, and make sure you're up and ready to go before sun-up tomorrow. I'll get the missus to bring some grub over for you.' Then he turned and walked back towards the big house, leaving me rolling a smoke and trying to take it all in.

The boss was prone to lead by action not words. That last long sentence of his was an unusually extended set of lectures from the big man. A short string of single syllables was normally a communicative day for Robert. He was a man who firmly believed in simplicity. Less was more for him, but this was in direct conflict with the actual size of the man, and he liked to wear an extra extra large classic American Stetson hat. Big as he was, his demeanor was not rough, and his attitude not as one might expect, considering the country he lived in. Rob had nothing to prove to anyone. Over the course of the next ten months he was efficient in words and action, and intimately connected with horse, cattle and the land.

I found the best room in the long row of rooms that made up the workmen's quarters, and organised the most comfy cot and the softest pillow. Then I consumed a huge plate of sausages and mash potato brought down to the quarters by Rob's wife, Ruby. I slept badly that night, thinking over the day. In the morning I was woken by a solid knock on my door at six-thirty am. The success of finding the suicide case and the prospect of a year of long grass and fat cattle had put Rob in an extraordinarily good mood for him to sleep in so late. For the rest of the season I was lucky to still be horizontal after five o'clock. When I opened my door Rob threw me the keys to the old Tojo again and told me simply, 'Elliott Store, ask for Mary.' Driving to Elliott to pick up perishables at the store or a couple of ringers or jackaroos looking for work at Murranji was to become a regular job for me over the season.

Luckily I had the nonce to check the oil and water, fill a jerry can with fuel and a large container of fresh water, and check that I still had the winch, towrope and wallaby jack. Heading off towards town with a warm sun topping the scrub, I watched a mob of station horses graze in the bottom corner of the front paddock. Twice I had to stop to blow the radiator cap and wait for twenty minutes for the old truck to cool down enough to continue, and two and a half hours later I pulled up in front of the Elliott Store. As I walked through the screen door into the shop a woman was yelling. 'Get out of here with that stinkin' roo you worthless piece of shit!' Then I met Mary.

Mary was a slight woman about fifty years old, but her small stature didn't match the size of her personality. She had a fondness for two things. One was using more than her fair share of derogatory expletives in every sentence. The other was her husband Ron, the very subject of her constant abuse. Ron and Mary had come to the Territory from Melbourne on a driving holiday years before, and never gone back. Their little shop provided ringers from local stations with hats and boots and leather and tobacco and magazines. They gave passing tourists advice about country driving and told them about the local attractions, like the pub next door and Lake Woods thirty kilometres to the south. They also supplied them with cool drinks and groceries, and if tourists wanted to try their luck at catching a fat yellow belly, they sold them bait and fishing rods.

Mary's temper was well known in town. She believed young people should show consideration to 'those of more mature standing,' and more than a few cheeky young jackaroos had felt the back of Mary's hand after not showing due respect. By contrast she had a soft spot for the local kids, and they loved her. She took stew and boiled veggies and cool drinks to their camp over behind the pub, and she'd talk to them about the benefits of reading and writing, and try to get them all busy to keep them off the grog. You didn't let on that you knew she has a softer side. That was a sure way to get your hat knocked off your head and a stern 'mind your own bloody business.'

The 'stinkin' roo' Mary had referred to as I walked into the store was the animal she'd asked Ron to bring inside and cut up for the dogs. Ron simply took the roo and the abusive tirade back outside to complete the job on the workbench at the back door. He simply said, 'Yes dear.'

Mary said, 'What the hell do you want, city boy?' as I walked in.

'Okay, that's it. I don't bloody understand it. What is it that gives me away? Wrong hat? Jeans not dirty enough? What?' I demanded.

Mary responded with a grin and a short, 'You'll find out.'

I handed over the shopping list and said, 'I'm working at Murranji. My name's Andy. Robert sent me for perishables.' Mary turned on her heel to fill out the order, leaving me standing in the shop, listening to Ron whistle as he cut the roo into bite-sized chunks.

On the way back to Murranji I thought about the horse-breaker, the wild bronc in the steel yards, the trackers and the suicide case. About the station manager and the pair at the store back in Elliott. Under a shady tree halfway back to the station while the Tojo's engine cooled down, I wondered if the last couple of days were normal up here. I knew I was going to have to concentrate and watch what I said and did.

The rough blokes who would come through the property weren't going to take any crap. When a job needed doing they'd expect me to jump in and do it, and conversation would be a luxury. If I said I could do something, I'd better make bloody sure I was really good at it because there was no doubt I'd be put to the test. I filled the tired old radiator once more and headed up the track to Murranji for the second time in as many days.

As I drove I squeezed the steering wheel really hard in a futile attempt to toughen up for the next round of heavy hand-shaking.

"The first seven years were the hardest when I first went out there in 1928, Humbert River Station was just a few bark huts...I took one look at it all and thought, "I'll be lucky to last a bloody year out here." I left Humbert forty-four years later.'

Beyond the Big Run,
Charlie Shultz 1998

CHAPTER 3
Settling In

Driving into the compound at dusk I went straight to the Big House. Rob told me which freezer to put the perishables in and I was given a bowl of camp stew Ruby had made. I put the Tojo to bed and wandered over to the workmen's quarters. The kitchen lights were burning and I could hear yelling and what sounded like crashing chairs. I put my dinner on the landing out front of the kitchen and slowly approached the door.

I had a quick glance around the corner of the doorway before putting my body in the firing line. Pots and pans flew around the kitchen, and the kitchen table and its chairs were scattered around the rough concrete floor. The man responsible for the noise and fuss was the man with the black hat from the previous day at the yards. 'I hate fucking rats,' he said with menace as he hurled another saucepan across the room. 'Bloody disease-carrying bastards. Those beady little eyes, I hate 'em.'

The rat came darting out from under the stove, took a swerve around the upturned table, and shot straight at the opening under my legs at the door. I ducked backwards, and the rat scooted over the doorstep as a pan came flying out, followed by an angry ringer with an egg flipper in his hand. He came back into the kitchen as I was putting the kitchenware back into cupboards and together we turned the dining table right side up and introduced ourselves.

'My name's Malcolm, but call me Mal. I'm head stockman here but don't let that worry you, I'm really a softy.' Mal was interested to find out what the suicide thing was all about. He'd seen the police jeep and the trackers, but he'd only squeezed a few details out of the boss. He said getting information out of Rob was like getting a ringer's last beer — 'Nearly impossible without a firearm.'

The two of us sat up for a couple of hours, rolling cigarettes while moths smashed themselves into two naked light bulbs hanging from the ceiling. We talked about my first day, the suicide case, the Murranji Track, the boss and the storeowners, and friends left behind. About girls, trips we'd done around the country, rodeos, and girls. I told Mal stories of growing up in Sydney, of air-conditioned shopping malls, over-crowded trains, and the hollow waves that peel off the southern end of Dee Why Point. I spoke of riding motorbikes and falling off surfboards. Mal told stories of driving cattle and falling of buck-jumpers.

I told him my grandfather had spent time as a young man on a cattle property in the middle of South Australia and because of the stories he told I knew that one day I was going to do it too. I'd spent hours reading cowboy books, and watching John Wayne movies, and knew that at some point I was going to drive away from the city and head north.

Mal said horses, droving and yard-work were all he'd ever done. He'd started as a jackaroo, worked hard at becoming first a ringer, and then a head stockman. He spoke of droving camps, and working on the railway, and breaking horses. He offered long explanations on how best to mouth a young colt, how to work with a green horse, and what to do when one 'drops its head.' He described how a good horse can make station life a joy, and how a great horse can change a man forever. Mal had what ringers call 'the gift.' That special sense with animals very few people possess. It's a way of feeling what a horse is thinking, of smelling what a horse is feeling. 'I can't really explain it, you just know,' he said. I had no idea, but I was willing to learn.

He was especially proud of 'Matchbox,' a horse he'd broken a couple of years earlier. Mal reckoned Matchbox could 'think like a cow.' During a muster the previous year when they were bringing a big mob back from Mud Bore to the main yards at the homestead Matchbox offloaded a young jackaroo into the dust when it jumped sideways and took off after a breakaway steer. The horse had been watching the animal as it worked its way to the edge of the mob, getting ready to gallop for the treeline. Mal laughed as he told the story, 'He didn't expect her to bolt so quick. And you should've seen her get around the steer all by herself.'

Finally Mal got up and headed towards his own quarters, and as he left he said, 'You've got a big day tomorrow. We'll pick you out a couple of nice ponies in the morning. They're gonna be your best friends for the next ten months.'

The night was quiet, but sleep didn't come quickly. All the ringers were due to start arriving that week and the workmen's quarters would never be so peaceful again. At least, not until the start of the next wet season when, like pelicans, the jackaroos and ringers would migrate south for Christmas, or north to Darwin to blow the cash they'd saved on beer and girls.

I was woken at five o'clock by a sound that became familiar at that hour; creaky fly-screen doors being thrown open and the boss's booming voice, 'Come On!' There was always a momentary expectation following the alarm. I wondered, 'Come On What? Come On Where?' I never had to wait very long to find out. Rob told me to, 'Get over to the workshop and see Mal.'

It was my third day on full pay, on a genuine outback cattle station. Mal was waiting in the workshop, uncomfortably astride an old red motorbike. 'I hate these bloody things' he said as I walked up. 'A motorbike is not like a horse, no sense of self-preservation.' I jumped on a dust-covered quad bike as Mal kicked his own two-wheeler into life, and we headed down to the front paddock to send in the station horse mob. Later that morning Mal's motorbike's accelerator stuck on wide open and he yelled as he abandoned ship to let the bike disappear into a thick stand of pea-bush. I went down later that day to retrieve the machine and bend its handlebars straight.

We ran the horses into the main yards and spent the rest of the day separating the good from the bad, the ugly, and the useless. Every ringer was going to get up to five each, and they'd be responsible for making sure their horses were fed and watered before they could think about finishing up for the evening. Ringers also had to trim their horses' feet daily and were expected to clean and grease their own saddles and tack.

Mal could tell the ability of a man by looking at him, so he picked out two stockhorses for me befitting my level of expertise — pony club dropout. Then it was time for saddle and tack. I was the first ringer on the station so I got the pick of the gear. A good thing too because I was going to be spending a hell of a lot of time sitting in the saddle, so I made sure it was a comfy fit.

When we rode out that afternoon for a short exploration across the plain stretching away from the main yards to the south, I felt like the King of the World. I recalled tedious hours staring out the windows of airless classrooms dreaming of the bush and clear skies, and hours working at a dead-end job to save enough money for the trip. Now it was real, and I was trotting out towards the desert astride a big brown stockhorse with the outback sun on my back and a flock of black cockatoos screeching across the sky.

The next morning the boom of the boss's voice woke me from a deep and peaceful sleep. I leapt out of bed and grabbed some dry bread and a handful of Vita-Wheat biscuits as I rushed out the door and onto the back of the waiting truck. I decided right then to make sure to get out of my cot in the mornings well before anyone came shouting, so I could toast my bread and spread some Vegemite on my Vita-Wheats. After a short while I got so used to waking up at four thirty that it took me years to get back into a 'normal' routine.

A ringer tailing a small mob of Murranji cross-breds – mostly brahman and short-horn steers.

We drove down to the yards in the dim light. The air was surprisingly cold, and the noises around me already familiar. From the back of the truck I could hear the horses whinnying and pawing around the yards. Two of the blackfellas from that first day in the yards, Garry and Jimmy, were already busy in the breaking yard with a big chestnut gelding as we pulled up. I followed Rob and Mal, ready for anything. Rob went down to check the gates, the cattle race and the loading ramps while Mal and I saddled up.

The two horses allocated to me were named 'Big John' and 'Brolga.' Big John was a bay gelding that stood tall at the wither, and Brolga was a big chestnut gelding with half of one ear missing. They were perfect choices for me because they were cattle-smart, and they'd forgotten how to buck. Many times over the next few months, while riding the flank with a mob of cattle or while 'tailing' a mob to settle them down in preparation for yard work, I'd successfully chase a breakaway back into the mob. I'd whoop and whistle as I rode as if I knew what I was doing, but in fact it was the horse that could see what was happening long before I awoke to the idea.

Brolga came straight up to me that morning as I jumped down into the holding yard. He sniffed my hat, and I patted his cheek as I spun a lead rope around his neck like an amateur. If working in the outback was graded like martial arts, then I was a white belt beginner. I was a jackaroo in training, and a jackaroo is a ringer in training, a ringer being an Australian stockman. I had a long way to go to earn the title, to become competent with horses, cattle, fencing, mustering and yard work. To learn the skill of cutting a young bull's balls out without making it bleed too much, and to work in close contact with large angry cattle in hot dusty yards without getting myself or anyone else killed.

Later I took Big John for a quick ride southwest out towards Number 4 Bore, and I thought about how much my horse looked like those hundreds I'd seen years ago on a documentary about the Australian Light Horse — the men who sailed to Egypt in 1914 with their horses, their best mates. For those young Diggers it was a strange country, a strange culture and an unfamiliar night sky. But for me it wasn't 1914, and I couldn't imagine what it could have been like for them to be ordered to shoot their horses, five minutes after victory was declared, and then go home.

I didn't want to think about the end of the season at Murranji, the day in November when I'd have to repack my ute and drive away. I'd have to leave behind my mates, and the horses I'd spent the year getting to know.

Lots of people came through Murranji over the '87 season. Most years up to eight ringers and jackaroos turned up at Elliott by bus or car or on foot. They'd be brought to the station and introduced to their room, their horses, and saddle. Some stayed for months, some for the whole season. Others worked for a few weeks and they'd move on to other jobs, other stations. Some knew Murranji intimately and came back every year, but then there were others who didn't ever fit in — men who were all talk and no action, or who liked to drink too much, and some who just liked to fight. Murranji had a share of them all.

While the whitefellas slept in the workmen's quarters provided, the blackfella-stockmen camped with their families down by the dam on the other side of the homestead, cooking tucker over open fires and generally kept to themselves. Jimmy, Garry and other blackfellas spent most of their spare time there. On the odd occasion after I'd knocked off from a day's riding I'd walk down to the camp with Garry, and we'd sit around poking the fire, making coffee and rolling cigarettes. We'd laugh together and swap stories about bastard cattle, or getting kicked in the yards, or riding flat out through scrub chasing breakaways. If he knew I had no idea what I was talking about, he never let on.

Sometimes lost tourists arrived, or neighbours needing rolls of fencing wire or a chat. Twice a travelling library bus visited. We'd pick out tattered paperback westerns and if there was no television, or no one willing to lose at poker, we'd read them between dinner and the sack. A couple of Christian preachers turned up to save our souls, and a travelling salesman arrived in a colourful kombi van to relieve us of our spare cash. The salesman did okay at Murranji that year. He knew a ringer couldn't survive without a good pocketknife and leather pouch, a big shiny belt buckle, a fancy silver-buttoned cowboy shirt and a pair of Cuban-heeled riding boots. For two days after the kombi drove away we looked like a herd of midnight cowboys, but we soon got caked in dirt and cow shit and the dusty look returned.

Flying vets, and 'Stockies' (Stock Inspectors), appeared out of the sunrise to test the mobs for diseases as part of a government disease eradication program, and sometimes the Elders stock and station agent flew in with cattle-buyers to check Rob's latest mob, sell him drums of a new type of drench, or share the latest gossip from town.

One old man arrived early in the season with a bedroll, a billycan and an interesting lot of shoeing tools in an old leather bag. His skin was leathery and his teeth brown. He smoked rollies continuously, and always sounded like he was about to cough up a lung. He'd walked into the Territory in 1954, but had no idea how old he was. He remembered a childhood of drover's camps in Queensland, of learning to ride bareback before he knew the alphabet, and getting a job as a cook for a team of ringers before ever spending a day in a schoolhouse. He was around fifty, but he looked closer to seventy, but if you added up all the years, from all the stories he told of all his experiences and conquests he'd made, he had to be closer to one hundred and five. His name was Ray and he had a profound impact on me.

Ray had a huge reputation as a saddler and an expert horseman, and the best horse-breaker around. He showed the crew on Murranji how to work leather, to fix saddles and make a rope bridle. He taught us how to look after our horses and he demonstrated how to get in close to the horse's flanks when working on its hooves.

Ray did most of the shoeing at Murranji, and I helped him whenever I could. I held the horses' lead rope and tried to sooth it as Ray worked away at speed with rasp and nippers and shoeing nails. Ray could sense when a horse was going to kick out with the leg he was working on because he could feel it tense up. He'd quietly lift the leg away from his body, and the horse would kick with no impact. He knew when a horse was going to buck, and he knew when it was finished bucking from the look in its eyes or feel it in its muscles. 'It's all about the feeling,' Ray said, 'You can't teach that.'

'Bloody pity,' I said, longing to understand.

When nobody was looking I walked up to one of the horses, ran my hand down the wither, over the flank, down the leg to the crook just above the hoof, and lifted. I pulled, tugged and squeezed. 'There must be a trick,' I thought as I struggled with the leg. Then 'boom,' I got kicked in the thigh and went sprawling on the ground.

One Sunday morning when I was in the workshop fixing a flat tyre on my ute, Ray walked up and leant on the tray. 'You ever get lucky in the back there?' he asked, gesturing to the back of the ute while making a rollie. 'Only in my dreams,' I replied. Ray noticed the rusty dog chain hanging from the rail that ran along under the back window, and asked, 'Where's your pan-licker?'

The question brought back bad memories. I'd only recently lost my dog, my best mate. 'It happened on the way up here,' I said to Ray. 'He was a tough little red heeler dog, but he was nearly human.'

I got 'the red dog' as a pup about a year before I left Sydney. We spent every minute together travelling all the way up the east coast to Cairns. Most nights I cooked in the coals of an open fire, and we camped under a tarp strung to a tree. At night the dog slept with one eye open and one ear cocked. He'd come over to my swag in the middle of the night and lick my face to wake me if something moved near the camp. When I met people in our travels I had to introduce them to the red dog first. It was prone to taste someone's calf muscle if provoked and sometimes when not, so I had to make sure the dog was comfortable with strangers before I could shake their hands. We looked after each other, and I thought we'd spend years together fetching sticks and chasing cattle. But that wasn't to be.

I told Ray about Mt Isa. About the crows, the snake and the tears. We'd arrived at about lunchtime and set up camp next to a dried creek bed just outside town. The red dog was asleep under the ute as I went about setting a fire, when all of a sudden it was yelping and thrashing about under the car. As I ran over I wondered what the bloody hell had set the dog off that way. It must have been a snake. A bastard snake.

I bent down and saw the dog had its head caught in the leaf springs on the back axle. It was thrashing about and starting to tear skin away from its jaw. I grabbed the car jack from out of the tray and shoved it under the side door. I knew if I could raise the chassis off the axle the leaf springs would open up, and the dog could come free. But the jack broke and I looked around frantically for something I could use to lever the weight of the car off the dog.

An old tree had fallen next to the creek bed so I grabbed a long sturdy branch and ran back. The yelping was getting worse and each yelp sounded like someone punching me in the guts as I shoved the branch under the ute and strained to lift it a couple of inches. The dog came flying out with teeth bared and a crazy look in its eyes. After a year of happy times, of eating the same meals, and walking the bush, I couldn't believe what was happening. The red dog was going mad. It went for my throat and I had to hit him down, then stand and watch as he thrashed around, snarling and vomiting.

The dog's back legs stopped working and he slowly settled down. I knelt heavily down beside him and watched as his eyes turned blue. I would always remember that colour. I stood up and mechanically pulled the .22 out from behind the seat of the ute, and loaded it with one shell. The red dog was nearly gone. Its breathing was heavy and slow as I pulled back the dog's lips and saw that the colour was gone from his bare gums. I fired, then cried.

The ground was hard, but I scratched with a camp shovel as I watched crows starting to circle around the campsite. I hated those crows. 'You're not going to have him,' I said. I buried my red dog in a shallow grave beside the dry creek bed near Mt Isa that day, then drove west for three hundred kilometres, wanting to get as far away as quickly as I could.

As I told Ray this story the old saddler stood quietly smoking, considering the tale. There was a pause as he thought about it again. Then Ray said softly before strolling down towards the yards, 'Bloody snake.'

Yep, bloody snake.

'The population of the district consisted of station managers, cattle duffers, horse thieves, wild and woolly stockmen and outlaws.'

Beyond the Big Run,
Charlie Shultz 1998

CHAPTER 4
Tough Up There

I drove into Elliott every couple of days over the next three weeks to pick up jackaroos and ringers off the bus from Alice or Katherine. They were easy to spot with their loud shirts, dusty riding boots and wide-brimmed hats. They wore leather belts threaded through scuffed jeans, with pouches of different shapes and sizes for pocketknives, tobacco and matches. Their bedrolls, backpacks and duffel bags were covered in a fine layer of dust.

Mitch, a mechanic from Melbourne, arrived at Murranji in his own truck during the second week. He'd been travelling around the country for many years but was up in the Territory to see what the Top End had to offer. He said he was in-between jobs and in-between girlfriends, 'But on the lookout for both.' Mitch's LandCruiser had a full set of tools in steel racks in the back — a big collection of spanners and sockets in a huge bright red cabinet, a portable generator, stick welder, and an oxy-acetylene set.

Chris turned up on the last day of March. His family had moved from Tonga to Townsville when he was ten years old. He had a knack for reading your mind when you were playing poker and another knack of suddenly disappearing when the boss was looking for someone to dig a posthole, or chop firewood, or some other chore. Chris didn't like being indoors so he slept out most nights on an old cot on the veranda. Sometimes he rolled his swag out on the lawn in front of the workmen's quarters and slept under the stars. He tied a piece of mozzie mesh from his swag to the top of a steel post with some baling twine to keep bugs off his face, and fell asleep. His snoring added to the night noises, as constant as the faint hum from the diesel generator in the little shed behind the workshop.

Other ringers appeared on Murranji over the following days. Dave from Darwin and Martin from Alice Springs arrived in Elliott on separate buses and went straight to the pub. I had a couple of beers with them, then bundled them into the Tojo for the trip out to the station. Dave was thick and burly, and Martin thin and surly. They didn't talk much about where they came from or how they got to Murranji, and I got the idea I wasn't supposed to ask.

The Territory was a great place to go if you wanted to earn a bit of money, get two (sometimes three) square meals a day and a cot, and not be asked too many questions. Station bosses needed labour and men needed work. No references or tax forms required.

I was enjoying myself immensely. There was a sense that something was building, that we were preparing for something big. When I wasn't driving to town and back I was pitching in around the homestead, and I hadn't stuffed up, yet. I helped Mitch service the tractors and trucks, and spent long hours helping pull gearboxes, differentials and axles out of the station vehicles on the diesel-stained workshop floor.

A number of blackfella-stockmen drove themselves out to Murranji in beat-up topless Toyotas, with a group of family members on-board. They parked at the camp down below the homestead and settled in for the season. Appearing and disappearing at various times over the course of the season, they kept to themselves most of the time but they were not unfriendly, they simply stayed busy and didn't seem to want to talk much.

Early in the third week I drove to Elliott to pick up 'Rusty' from down south, and a big fella called 'Mungo.' Mungo's hair was curled as tightly as a Brilo pad, and his big hands had fingers like fat sausages. Close to twenty stone, he took up more then his share of the bench seat in the Tojo so Rusty sat on his swag in the back and covered his face with a shirt to keep the dust out of his mouth and eyes. We headed northwest to Murranji and as usual we stopped halfway and sat around listening to the radiator hiss as it cooled down.

While we waited Mungo explained that he came from an island in the Pacific. His family had moved to Australia when he was small and he'd been drifting around, working here and there, for about ten years. He was large in stature and huge in appetite. Rusty carried a swag and a backpack full of clothes, Mungo had a bedroll and a big plastic carry bag full of junk food and soft drinks. Rusty said he was working his way around the Top End — a couple of weeks here and there, then on to the next rodeo or dance to blow his money on bull riding, beer and women. He explained that most of the time his money would be wasted on the first two, and he'd get too pissed to spend any on the third. I showed them both to their own rooms in the workmen's quarters and then showed them the yards.

On one trip I picked up a couple of blackfellas from the camp behind the pub. They didn't talk much, but one of them had a guitar and the other an old harmonica with two notes that didn't work properly. I heard a funny squeak now and then when the harmonica player tried to slide past a bad note and jump to the next one. The bloke holding the guitar was Walter. He took charge of all the indigenous riders at Murranji and they followed his lead, especially when they started to sing. They sang Slim Dusty tunes such as 'Camooweal' and 'Ringer from the Top End,' and the harmonica player, Peter, took the squeaky instrumental parts. Peter had the biggest Stetson hat that I'd ever seen. He told me he'd once seen a documentary about tropical birds of paradise that adorned themselves with colours and leaves to enhance their manhood, and attract a mate. He said with a sly wink and a friendly pat on the shoulder, 'It works for them and it works for me.'

I enjoyed the trips to town. I loved driving and it meant I had one of the more important jobs at the station during this early part of the season. Picking up perishables and other assorted equipment and machinery parts from the Elliott store I became friends with the storeowners, and I knew most of the regulars at the Elliott Hotel. The pub was a great place to catch up on gossip and join in important conversations about the weather, the difference between tap beer and bottled beer, and current cattle prices.

Sometimes I didn't get away from Murranji for an Elliott run until late afternoon, so on top of all the necessary tools, supplies and eskies required for the trip, I threw in my swag to sleep out on the track. I spent evenings talking with ringers from other stations and challenging jackaroos from the nearby Kerry Packer-owned spread, Newcastle Waters Station, to serious games of eight ball on the pool table. I chatted to passing truckies and tourists who were quenching their thirsts as they travelled the Stuart Highway.

The Elliott Hotel had bits of old leather and rusty tools hanging from the ceiling, and photos of winning racehorses spread around the walls. The bar had deep scratches where ringers have carved their names and dates to commemorate their drunken visits, and the stools were made of wicker cane and covered in green vinyl. Two big ceiling fans rotated slowly, and a battered old baseball bat hung on a hook just behind the publican's shoulder.

Elsewhere in Australia it may have been 1987, but in this part of the country it was still 1947. The Hotel had two bar rooms but there was no sign over the doorway separating the two. No signs that announced any title or signified any cultural shift, but you just knew the 'other' bar was where the blackfellas could spend their money. The front bar was adorned with framed pictures of landscapes on the walls and there were nice drink coasters on the bar. The other bar had a pull-down cage, a pool table with no felt left, and chairs that were screwed down where they sat.

Rules were different up there. The publican proudly pronounced to me one night that the Northern Territory was tough country and, 'You have to be tough to survive.' Relationships were uncomplicated and problems were sorted out quickly. If you had an issue with someone you took it outside, you sorted it out, and then you came back inside and kept drinking. Except for cards and pub pool, there was little time for games. There wasn't room for precious complications and people enjoyed simplicity. Most things in the Territory were still very 'black and white.'

One night while I was sitting at the bar having a quiet drink with Ron after the store had closed for the evening, a frail little blackfella came rushing in and sat down with a wheeze next to the jukebox in the corner. An angry woman came bursting in right behind him, and she was brandishing what looked like an old axe handle, luckily without the steel head. She was screaming words didn't understand, but I could see that the cowering bloke by the jukebox was grasping every word. I never saw anyone take such a pounding — three great swings of the axe handle — and survive, let alone keep pleading. Then the local cop burst in, grabbed the weapon away from the woman and dragged the man to his feet. Like a couple of kids the two yelled abuse at each other, separated by the extended arms of the copper who was explaining that a night in the lockup was going to cool them down a bit.

Everyone was getting bundled outside to be processed when two drunk ringers decided it was their turn to get physical, so they started smashing each other with a couple of those nice cane stools. It was more like the wild west than I was used to so I decided to exit the pub at that point, showing a surprising mental ability directly disproportionate to the amount of alcohol I had consumed that evening. I slept in my swag on the back of the Tojo and woke the next morning to a peaceful town. Grabbing the supplies from the Elliott Store I headed out to Murranji to see what next she had to offer.

Something didn't seem right as I walked towards the yards. The men were acting weird. It was mid-morning and they should have been busy drafting or otherwise pushing cattle around, but all the ringers were leaning on rails at various points around the yards and Ray was perched in the car seat on top of the race. Mal was standing in the round yard holding the reins on a big ugly horse that I'd noticed never got any attention. That was, until now.

Dave called over from the other side of the yards, 'Come on city boy, we've got you a ride.' I knew something was up as I jumped the rails of the round yard. I walked over to Mal who didn't look me in the eye as he handed me the thick green-hide reins. The horse seemed quiet. 'No problem,' I thought. 'Piece of cake,' I said quietly to myself as I grabbed some mane and planted my left foot firmly in the nearside stirrup. Mal held the bridle as I swung my leg over quickly and sunk as deep and tight into the saddle as I could. Mal said quietly, 'Keep your arms loose and your hands tight,' as he let go and backed away.

Nothing happened, and nobody moved. I gave the horse a jab with my heels and walked him around the yard. The horse just walked on, breathing evenly. No worries.

Mal nodded at Walter who opened the big gate to the main yard, the horse spotted freedom and jumped full length for the gate. Luckily I had a handful of mane or I would've been left suspended in mid-air. I crashed back down into the saddle as the horse hit the ground and pig-rooted into its front legs. The next thing I felt was the back of my head hitting the horse's rump and then my hat flying off my head when my face hit the leather of the bridle between the ears on the horse's head. I hit the dirt, face first. I dusted myself off as I stood up and stomped over to pick up my hat. Still nobody moved, but they were watching closely.

Ray looked down at me with questioning eyes, wondering what I was going to do next. I walked over to the big ugly horse standing quietly next to the rails with a cheeky bloody grin on its face, grabbed the reins up and started back towards the round yard. As I walked past Mal I quietly asked, 'What's its name Mal?'

'Bundy, Buckjumping Bundy,' was his cheeky reply.

I knew I was being tested. If I got back on this firecracker I was going to be right for the rest of the season — I'd be able to play with the big boys. If not, I might as well pack my things and drive away right then. I'd seen it happen at school, and on fishing trawlers and in packing sheds. It would happen again and again later in life in office meetings, at pubs, and at parties.

As I turned the horse around and closed the big steel gate through which I'd just flown I wondered if men were the same all over the world. Testosterone may be a necessary hormone to help young boys become men, but it does strange things to a male brain. The need to compete, to test out your mettle. I got back on and tightened my grip once more. The arches of my boots pushed hard into the base of the stirrups, my thighs felt the leather of the pommel at the front of the saddle, and the hairs on the back of my neck were tingling. But I was ready this time.

'Righto Walter, open the gate!' I yelled.

Then all hell broke loose. The horse rooted, bucked and lunged for the gate, and all the men started yelling and cheering. Mal was yelling like a madman, 'Tuck 'im in' he shouted and, 'lean into 'im.' Even Ray added loud advice, 'Lean back when he kicks out.' Garry was clapping and whistling, and the other ringers were shouting advice and yelling helpful obscenities. Everything was suddenly really clear, and time slowed. With my knees I gripped the saddle with the strength of two men, and I tried to twist my body and throw my arm backwards in the same way I'd seen Garry do it that first day in the yards. The whole episode lasted about four seconds before I again tasted Territory dust. I was dragged to my feet and clapped on the back and told, 'Better luck next time,' and, 'Great ride son,' and, 'You nearly bloody had him that time.'

Nobody called me 'city boy' after that.

'..my tongue was starting to stick to the roof of my mouth and my throat felt like a rusty rasp when I heard the sound of a horsebell straight ahead..... inside another mile I found myself back at the gate I had left five hours earlier.'

Measures of a Mis-spent Youth, Packhorse and Pearling Boat,
Tom Ronan 1964

CHAPTER 5
BETTER MAN

By April a routine had set in. For weeks we'd get up before the sun, eat some Weet-Bix or toast, and head down to the yards to saddle up for the day. We'd ride out to Mud Bore or Number 4 Bore and muster a mob to the big steel yards back at the homestead. By the third day I had a pretty good idea of what I was meant to do. I knew where to stand, when to push, when to grab a gate, and when not to jump into a busy yard. The boss was always watching and he'd tell the jackeroos to 'bring 'em up steady.' Rob didn't want to rush the cattle, he preferred them as quiet as possible — they were easier to handle that way.

Half of the ringers spent the morning drafting off the young bull calves and heifers (the weaners) from the cows and putting the old bulls over the back into the big holding paddock. The other half started the branding fire, organised the marking gear, greased up the cradle and started pushing the first mob up so the young males could get the 'quick snip.' The cleanskins were branded and the whole lot were vaccinated, tagged and got the special Murranji earmark.

The yards were noisy with whistles and ringers' voices coaching the cattle through gates, and every so often an urgent yell of 'Look out!' when a cow chased a ringer or two. I quickly learnt to keep the bulls separated in the yards because at nearly a tonne they're not going to give a second's thought to a rowdy little jackaroo waving a plastic stick when there's a score to settle, and a harem to defend. The ground shook when their huge bodies clashed, pushing each other across the ground and into the yard's corner posts.

The low grunts of disturbed bulls and the constant bawling of cows separated from their calves became the soundtrack for life at Murranji. It was hard work and the yards were dusty and hot, but it was fun. Most ringers choose to act like idiots at any opportunity, and it helped to break up the long hot busy days. Every day had laughs and a little pain — you haven't lived until you've had a half-tonne bullock stand on your toes or a cow kick you in the nuts so hard you think your nose will bleed.

My first few weeks riding at Murranji were pretty tame. Nice short hops out to muster mobs of two hundred or more, mother them up and hold them on open ground about a kilometre from the homestead. Hours spent tailing cattle, educating them, pushing them here and there and settling them into a quiet mob near the yards, getting them ready for drafting. But then came my first big muster. The others were talking about it for days. Everyone was going to be riding out past Number 10 Bore to the north, and my bum was never going to be the same.

The day before the muster began was spent greasing saddles, organising gear, dressing hooves, and packing gear for the big drive. Mal got me to help him with the boss's horses, Shotgun and Sandy. I'd never seen horseflesh like them — big chestnut stockhorses with muscles on muscles across their chests and broad rumps. They held their heads high and were always twitching as if some kid was constantly poking at them with a stick. They lived in luxury in stables behind the big house and they got the full treatment from Ray, with special attention to teeth and shoes.

In the morning it was all action. Everyone got fed early with big plates of eggs and bacon on thick slices of freshly cooked, crusty damper. We packed our swags onto the back of the trucks, organised water bottles and full tobacco tins. We'd be away from the homestead for about three days, and the plan was to muster some of the paddocks to the northeast and bring calves and cows back to Murranji's main yards for the full treatment. We rode away just after sunrise.

Six hours later I thought my pants were on fire. I'd never ridden for so long or so far. That was the last time in my life that hair grew properly on the inside of my legs below my knees. That evening we sat around the fire talking about the ride. I preferred to lie on my stomach on top of my swag and Jimmy offered me some pale brown goo for my sore skin. He squeezed it through his fingers into my open palm.

I wasn't sure about the goo but I was told it was the 'real deal' and I'd learnt that it was wise to listen to the blackfellas when it came to bush skills. They taught me how to find water in the scrub by digging in just the right place under a certain type of tree, and how to navigate at night. They gave useful survival tips like what plants and reptiles were good eating, and which ones could kill you or make you vomit for days. I put some of the paste on the raw skin of my legs and snuck some down the back of my jeans. It seemed to dull the pain somewhat. Ray said wisely, as if it was going to cheer me up, 'It'll get worse before it gets better, but it will get better.'

I was a little embarrassed to learn later that the special bush goo I'd been given was a dollop of Johnson and Johnson Intensive Care from the medicine pack in the truck, mixed with a pinch of red dust. No wonder the other ringers were sniggering a little more than usual that evening. 'It's too easy to play a trick like that on new recruits,' I thought.

As we rode out of camp the next morning the pain was worse than before. But after a short break around lunchtime it wasn't too bad, and was never a problem again. We came to a steel gate in an endless fence line, and one of the riders jumped off and pulled the gate back. The riders went through, the boss went through, the truck went through and the gate was shut behind the group. We milled around and waited for directions, leaning forward on our saddles. I looked at the horizon, broken here and there by stands of tall scrub. One long fence line stretched to the northeast, the other end out of sight behind us.

Rob stood in his genuine American saddle atop his big chestnut, then he looked around at the group and said, 'Right men, we're gonna muster this paddock today. I want 'em all in by mid-afternoon. Mal, you know what to do.' With that he started off down the fence line to northeast. All I could see was a fence line in two directions. How would it be possible to spread out so far and not get lost? Mal started explaining the job at hand as we headed off after the boss. He said we'd follow the fence line northeast and every so often one of the riders would break away to the west. He told everyone to keep the next bloke in their line of sight or in hearing range of their stockwhips, and that way we should be able to circle the whole paddock and bring back the cattle we found. What I didn't know till later was that the paddock was a hundred square kilometres and had around eight hundred cattle grazing in it!

By the time it was my turn to break off from the group and head in a wide arc to the west we were riding through thick scrub. I quickly got totally lost, alone, and back at the fence. I had no idea where the others were and little idea what to do next. I spent a couple of hours riding around in big circles and luckily happened to find my way back to the steel gate through which we'd all come, and waited there.

The first groups of ringers started to appear from the setting sun, each with a small mob of cows and calves and the odd steer or bull. I heard the far-off cracking of stockwhips and the faint yells of the ringers as they persuaded the cows along. As they came into view they yelled at me, 'Help 'em through!' I rode out in an arc around the mob and helped push them through the gate, and then helped hold them in a mob in the paddock on the other side. I was glad I wasn't a total waste of eggs and bacon that day.

We took it in turns to tend the cattle that night. Some of us slept in swags around the campfire or on the back of the trucks while others slowly rode around the mob. Cattle have a tendency to be jumpy after being chased around all day so a little human company at night helps settle them down. The next day we got the last of the stragglers organised and headed the mob for the portable yards. The weaners were drafted off and by lunchtime we had all the cattle sorted.

I saw a big dust cloud rising out of the southeast. Mal said it was the road train coming to pick up the mob. We watched it coming for about twenty minutes before it arrived, a Mack Superliner, fifty metres long with three huge cattle trailers. Fully loaded it could weigh one hundred and twenty tonnes. As it thundered along the third trailer was entirely obscured by the rising dust storm thrown up by the leading two trailers. Mitch the mechanic said quietly, awestruck by the sight and sound of its exhaust stacks, 'Four hundred horsepower...oooh.' It came barreling along the track and up to the yards, and then the driver expertly positioned the trailers in line with the loading ramp.

We squeezed the mob into the endless, low-roofed pens of the trailers. Yelling and prodding we persuaded the cattle with the sound of our whistles and the touch of our stockwhips. I only got kicked in the goolies twice that day. A bit of pain, a lot of gain. Chris once again scored the cushy job of looking after all the horses, while the rest of us pushed and cajoled the wild cattle through the tight yards and up the loading race. I'd get the cushy job another day, maybe.

The whole group worked with purpose, like a crack battalion on the move. Ray and Mitch followed behind the muster picking up the youngest of the calves and throwing them onto the back of the truck for a free ride, with their mothers trotting and bawling alongside. Sometimes I'd lean down off my saddle, pick up a small calf by the front legs and lean it across my horse's neck to give its young legs a break. As lunchtime approached Mitch and Ray drove ahead to the campsite, set a fire and put the billy on for a much-needed cuppa. Mitch organised the camp, the cooking fire and the meals, and Ray helped tend the horses' hooves.

Every day I was feeling more a part of the team. Over the months I got better at mustering in the long paddocks. I learned how to crack my stockwhip properly and gained the ringer's sense of knowing where I was supposed to be. So long as you were watching and listening as you went along you picked it all up after a while. One day I overheard Ray describe me to Mal as 'One of the jackaroos,' and I knew I was on the improve then. For the rest of the season I found it all pretty straightforward. We worked, ate and slept, then got up the next morning and did it all again. Simple.

On the fifth day of the first big muster we'd emptied another long paddock — healthy maiden country that grew fat bullocks. The cattle stood in a loose mob close by as a couple of ringers walked their horses slowly in a wide arc on the other side. It was late afternoon and I could hear the last of the mobs coming in. I was sitting easily in my saddle on the back of Big John, next to the boss's truck. Rob's horse Shotgun was tethered to the back of the truck, the shiny clips and buckles of its saddle glinting in the sun and the stirrups jingling each time the horse shifted its weight. Mitch was lazily making another rollie in the front seat and Rob was sitting on a log twenty yards away quietly talking with Walter about the muster. Everything was normal, quiet.

Then Shotgun bolted. Mitch had jumped out of the front seat and for some reason decided to slam the door with force. Shotgun shied from the sound and pulled back on the reins of his bridle. The horse leaned back so hard its hooves slid in the dust and then the reins snapped with a 'twang.' I was closest when it happened. Shotgun flew past me with the stirrups of the saddle kicking his flanks and the broken reins slapping him around his ears and neck, so I took off after him. I didn't know why I took off after him, I didn't really think about it. I just did it. And Big John seemed keen to go for a run.

It never occurred to me that galloping after a bolting horse was not the action of the brightest spanner in the toolbox, but there was nothing in the jackaroo's operating manual about this one. No previous words of advice from anyone about what to do if your boss's most prized possession decides to bolt towards the desert. I simply reacted. I wasn't to know the horse would probably pull up sooner or later, and then someone could ride up quietly and bring him back. Oh no, not me. I was going to chase him down as if I was Buck Rogers, as if I'd been riding for years.

As I gingerly reached out for Shotgun's broken reins with a bouncing, unsteady hand (at full gallop over rough rocky ground, with very little idea about what I was doing) the thought briefly crossed my mind that my present course of action might not be prudent, considering my less-than-average skill level. Luckily for me my antics were cut short by my own horse (the significantly smarter one of the working pair that day) who decided it was time to stop running so hard after the obviously much younger, faster and fitter animal. We came to a stop pretty quickly after that. Rob and mal turned up momentarily in the boss's truck and Rob yelled at me to, 'Stop fooling around and get back to the bloody mob.'

Another lesson learned, another punctuation mark in my travels through life. Then I saw another one, a weird one. I wasn't sure I was seeing right. I'd started back towards the mob when coming out of a stand of scrub just up ahead was a steer with flippers! Yep, flippers. It had what looked like a long flipper attached to each of its four hooves. I got closer and it took off towards the mob. It flew. It had extra speed. It kind of floated along. The other ringers saw it coming and they gathered around to have a closer look.

It turned out the steer was afflicted with a rare hoof disease which made each hoof grow at extraordinary speed. They grew faster than they were being worn down. Each 'flipper' was about a foot long and it gave the steer the ability to spring like an Olympic hurdler. We roped the steer down and rasped off the excess toe on each hoof, then let it up to rejoin the mob. We roared with laughter as the steer fell over a couple of times, trying to get used to having normal feet. I never forgot the day I met 'Twinkle Toes.'

Over the next two days we walked the remaining cattle back to the main yards at the homestead. The we gave the horses a wash down and let them go. They all enjoyed a roll in the dust, grunting and farting as they rolled on their sides and pawed the ground kicking up dust. As I slipped the bridle from Big John's head and he whinnied as if saying goodbye, and trotted over to the dam with the others. We put all the gear away in the tack room and settled back into the kitchen, exhausted and spent. I ate more than my share of camp stew then rubbed more of that special bush goo into my sore, but slightly stronger, hands.

For most of us, the next few days involved long hours tailing cattle, educating the weaners and pushing mobs around. For the others it was gardening, maintenance and servicing vehicles. We oiled saddles, greased gear and helped Mitch in the workshop. Some of the steel gates and yard panels needed welding and one hundred yards of fence needed replacing along the front paddock near the homestead. It was Martin and Rusty who got the fencing job, and this was a problem because they seemed to hate each other. They were always arguing about something — the best way to break a horse, or Holden versus Ford, or who had won the most number of fights. They must've been pretty close on that score because they appeared one evening in the quarters with an even number of bruises on each of their faces and knuckles — at least they'd sorted that one out and were pretty quiet with each other from then on. Then one morning Rob came down with Mal and Peter, picked me up and said, 'Let's go get dinner.'

The freezers were nearly empty. The last of the meat had been made into stew and the corned beef and mince sausages were nearly gone. We drove quietly across to the house mob in the airstrip paddock and Rob picked out a nice healthy-looking brown cow. I sat quietly on the back with Peter as we watched the shiny barrel of Rob's rifle slowly appear out of the driver's window. The cow was leisurely looking at us, chewing on that morning's grass.

Rob was a great shot and knew guns. They'd been part of his life since he was a kid, when there was always something to shoot — wild dogs, sick cows, brown snakes or dinner. The sound of the rifle shot was not as loud as I'd expected. I didn't think it was loud enough to kill anything, but I was quick to learn that it was not the power behind the shot that did the job, but rather the placement. Rob had shot true. He'd hit the sweet spot on the cow's forehead at the cross-point when you draw an imaginary line between each ear and the opposite eye.

I drew breath at how quickly the cow's lights went out. Her legs simply collapsed and she fell with a thud. Peter jumped off and ran to the beast with a knife, and the life gushed out of the beast and flowed across the dry ground in a shiny smear as he cut deep. We spread leaves across the tray of the ute and I helped ferry the big chunks of meat to the truck as the men's knives slashed and cut. Half an hour later and we drove away with a truckload of wobbling muscle — solid energy for hungry ringers.

All the meat was hung on hooks in the meat house for a couple of days and then we spent a morning slicing and dicing. We made corned beef and rolled roasts, and we minced the less-tender bits for sausages, bagging the whole lot as we worked and filling the freezer to the top. By lunchtime we were done and I wandered back to the quarters to get cleaned up.

Something was going on out front as I walked up. Mal was trying to teach Mitch how to use a stockwhip and everyone was standing around providing advice. Mitch was a wizard with sockets, spanners and impact drivers. He could trace an electrical circuit and pull injection systems apart, but when it came to things more supple, like animal leather and hide, he was at a loss. As I walked up, for the tenth time Mitch wrapped the stockwhip around his own neck with a 'thwap.' The ringers looked on sympathetically and laughed, and when Mitch finally gave up they gave him ten points for determination. As he walked back towards the workshop he told the onlookers he didn't have to get good at something he considered was never going to be 'core bloody business.'

And the others at Murranji never chided him too much about his lack of skill with horse or stockwhip. They knew his worth. They knew he was a key player in this outfit. If you were going to be driving an old station four-wheel-drive to one of the far-off bores, or miles across the property on some of the worst tracks in the area, you were glad when Mitch gave your truck some special treatment. You were happiest when he was along for the ride.

One day I broke a fuel line about fifty kilometres from the homestead. I'd gone out to service and refill an old diesel pump that ran one of the bores out there, and I was coming back when the Tojo broke down. I spent the night huddled in the passenger seat, and a lonely morning waiting for Mitch to realise I hadn't returned. Eventually Mitch grabbed a box of tools, some spares, and headed out to see 'what the bloody hell' was wrong. To Mitch, everything was 'bloody hell this,' and 'bloody hell that.' Good or bad. When Ray served up dinner he'd ask, 'What the bloody hell is this?' and he'd say, 'Why the bloody hell not,' when offered a beer. We got the truck going with a piece of rubber hose and some fencing wire. 'Fencing wire is so bloody handy' Mitch said when the engine fired into life.

On one trip to town for perishables I took Rusty to the bus stop to continue his trip around the Territory, and picked up his replacement — a little jockey from Adelaide. He looked okay when he got off the bus, nothing special, but it only took a couple of minutes for me to realise he was not going to fit in with the crew at Murranji. He talked non-stop, and most of it was annoying dribble about himself, his exploits, his theories about life, and the odd bad joke — followed by an annoying snigger. His boots were too shiny, he wore a bright yellow baseball cap, and he loved pointing out everything that was wrong with the world.

It was a long two-hour trip back to Murranji, and the jockey never stopped talking except to take a deep breath every now and then. After being annoyed with him, then angry with him, then annoyed again, I got bored, and he became like background noise on the trip. Like the noisy hum of the engine, his voice was a non-stop drone. I wondered if he ever took a break long enough to eat or sleep. Nope. He could eat and talk, work and talk, smoke and talk and yes, even at night I could hear the little jockey muttering to himself in his own room. Maybe he never slept? Nobody ever found out because nobody wanted to share a room with him. Nobody really ever wanted to be around him. I thought the other ringers might have tolerated him if he was half handy on a horse, but he was even lacking in that department. He couldn't get out of a trot without looking like he was about to fall off.

He was bundled into the Tojo the next time I took a trip to town. The others watched as we drove away with the noisy jockey snapping away in the passenger seat about how much better Mal could be if he only tried harder, and how old Ray had no idea about shoeing horses or what a bad boss Rob was. Nobody waved goodbye. After another three hours of hell I dropped the little jockey off at the bus stop in Elliott.

As I drove away I thought how lucky the jockey was to leave intact. I was amazed that one of the ringers hadn't choked him for some peace and quiet. Somehow he'd talked his way out of damage, and then amazingly kept on talking. You had to hand it to him though, he had energy. I took it as an example of what not to do. I remembered grandfather's voice, 'Travel through life with your eyes and ears wide open and you'll pick up enough tips to survive.' You take it all in, keep the good and chuck the bad.

CHAPTER 6
BLOODY UNFAIR

One morning in May started like most others. A quick cuppa, a piece of toast and then the boss', 'Come On!' We filed out of the kitchen and jumped onto the back of the Tojo, and trundled down to the yards for the umpteenth time that season. There were a hundred calves to mark and a mob of steers to load into a road train and kiss goodbye. Soon we'd be mustering out at the long paddocks at the far end of the property, but this day was to be another normal day in the main yards. Mungo was chewing on his seventh piece of toast as the truck rattled along, and Chris was twisting another cracker for his stockwhip when Mungo suddenly shoved him off the side into the pea-bush and tussocks. I hadn't heard what was said, but I guessed it must have been a cheeky jibe, enough to make the big fella take such action. Chris jumped up, dusted himself off, grabbed his hat and ran after the truck with the rest of us throwing stuff at him as he ran.

The cattle in the yards that day were a mob of crossbred steers. They were big and nervous, and cranky from being pushed around, and they tried to kill any ringer that came close. The yards were made of heavy gauge steel pipe, sturdy and tall because cattle like to try and push them over, or jump out.

When you were working in the noisy yards you had to be on your toes. You needed eyes in the back of your head — or at least you needed to know the bloke working alongside you was watching your back at the same time that he was watching his own.

It was dusty, hot and sweaty work. A cow might break out of a tight mob and come barreling at you, shaking its head with its nostrils flaring. I had to jump for the rails and get out of range many times every hour. I got used to it and started to expect it, predict it. Every now and then when I wasn't quite quick enough I'd get a little help getting up onto the top rail, a small patch of foamy cow's saliva on the back of my jeans.

And then you had the drafting yard where you really needed to be on your toes. It was shaped like a triangle with a narrow drafting gate at one end leading into the round yard. From there a beast could be sent any one of five directions, into other yards or up the loading race or dipping race — two long narrow corridors of steel, with sliding gates every two metres to stop the cattle pushing backwards. The drafting yard can only hold two big bulls, or three cows, or five big calves — and one nervous ringer. When working in the drafting yard you had to have one hand on the drafting gate, one hand holding a short piece of poly pipe (to persuade the cattle in the right direction), and one hand on the top rail in case you had to pull yourself up out of the way of an angry beast spinning around in front of you. This was the main problem for ringers working the drafting gate — only two hands, but three jobs to do. A couple of extra eyes would also have helped, and balls the size of coconuts a handy addition.

Ringers on the drafting gate job are not happy. There's no time for games in there. It's all business and concentration. Cows and calves come busting in, followed by an angry bull or a big steer with huge horns. You work them around and send the right one in the right direction. Then you have cattle in the round yard behind you that you've just drafted through. Sometimes they back up and kick the drafting gate and knock you into the mud if you aren't watching in that direction. It's no easy task. You can tell the cattle want to push you over into the mud and then step on your head as they run past. It's obvious in their eyes what they're thinking most of the time.

So it was that morning that I had a handful of drafting gate and sweat trickling down my inner thighs. It only took five minutes before thunder struck. I wasn't really switched on, I never was real good first thing in the morning. I managed to let a big bull through when it suddenly backed up and kicked the drafting gate with one of its powerful back legs. It did this just as I turned my head that way to see what was happening in the bull's direction. 'Crack!' the gate slammed into my face and I woke up a couple of seconds later flat on my back, looking up at the underside of a cow that was angrily stomping all over me.

Someone reached down and grabbed me by the shoulders, and I felt myself being dragged up and over the rails, and then landing with a thud in the dirt on the other side — the safe side. My nose felt funny. I thought, 'It's not supposed to move like that,' as I tugged it left and right. A tooth was loose, and my lip felt numb. Next thing I knew I was sitting hunched over the big table in the kitchen up at the workmen's quarters and Ray had the billy on. 'Looks like you bin' run over by a tractor,' Ray said as he pulled the old dusty mirror off the wall and handed it to me.

I didn't recognise the face looking back. The eyes were dark, the lips fat and the nose was bent and covered in blood. Mal and Chris were standing nearby making supportive comments like, 'Not so beautiful now is he,' and 'Don't worry mate, girls love scars.' Ray chased them out of the kitchen with a bread knife, telling them to, 'Get back down to the yards and do some work for once.' I wanted to go and get cleaned up but my legs didn't seem to be working. Ray said, 'Have a cuppa then go take a shower.' The tea was great and the shower was refreshing, that was until I passed out again and woke up on the tiled floor with a sore bum and water splashing my face.

Rob came up later and set my nose back in place with a shove of the heel of his right hand. Luckily he didn't warn me when he was going to do it, he just did it, real quick. He told me to relax for the next day and stay at the quarters. Forty-eight hours later and I was back to partially normal, back tailing cattle, working a mob. My cheek still feels funny at times, sometimes just before it rains, and my nose will carry a dent forever, but I consider it a reminder of my time in the Territory.

Ringers are supposed to look out for each other, watch each other's backs. The yards can get dangerous, dusty, noisy, hot and confusing. Cattle come at you from every direction. You might have a small mob in front, and a couple of angry cows behind, separated from their calves and not very happy about it. You have to know your mate in the yard with you is on the ball and watching what's happening.

Out of the dust and the noise the cow came at me — a medium-sized crossbred with yellow offset horns. I felt her on my arse before I heard her, and she hit me squarely, hard. I was young, and supple, so instinctively I flexed my legs and relaxed, and went with it. My feet touched the ground once before I was catapulted towards the rails, and I grabbed the top rail as she came in for a second hit. I tried to put a foot on a rail halfway up but it slipped through the gap and the cow hit me again while I was caught between the two rails. I felt my knee go 'snap' sideways, the wrong way.

The ringer in the yard with me that day (the bloke who was supposed to be watching my back) was a young bloke by the name of 'Phil.' Phil wasn't too handy around the yards, but he was a nice bloke, and Rob needed all the jackaroos he could get at this busy start to the season. A couple of days earlier I'd driven to town and picked Phil up from the bus. He'd come from Alice Springs and he said he'd been working on different properties around the Alice for a couple of years.

'Where the hell were you Phil?' I asked angrily. 'Why didn't you bloody sing out?' Phil didn't answer. I had a nagging feeling about Phil, but I wasn't sure what it was. That evening in the workmen's quarters I found out.

Phil was sitting quietly at the kitchen table with the other ringers. We'd just finished dinner and were playing cards and rolling cigarettes. Chris was fleecing Dave of his last thirty dollars and I was complaining about the pain as I rubbed oil into my sore knee. The oil was genuine goanna oil from a genuine goanna that Jimmy had caught earlier that day and rendered down the fat from its flanks. He'd given me the greasy oil in an old jam jar and told me to, 'Rub it in where it hurts. It'll fix it for sure.' The oil disappeared into my skin and sure enough, after a few days, the pain was gone.

Suddenly Phil swept cards and tin cups off the table with his arm as he fell heavily to the floor. Nobody moved for a second as they sat with surprise. Then Phil started to fit, violently shaking on the hard concrete. The ringers around the table had no idea what was happening, their forks poised halfway to their open mouths with bits of food falling back to their plates. But I knew, I'd seen it a hundred times before. I knew the signs, the slurred words, closed eyes. I knew the scary shakes, and the sweats.

I jumped down next to Phil and moved him onto his side as I yelled at the table for someone to get a wet tea towel, and someone else to get a pillow and a blanket. I knew that after the heat came the shivers. Mungo freaked out.

The sight of Phil possessed was too much for the big man and he ran out the kitchen door, yelling at the top of his lungs for Rob.

By the time the boss came into the kitchen things had settled down. Phil was sitting quietly at the kitchen table holding a blanket around his shoulders. 'How long have you been this way?' asked Rob. 'It comes and goes,' he replied softly. 'Station work is dangerous work,' said Rob as he turned and walked back to the main house to make some phone calls. He called the doctor to get more details about Phil's condition, and his contact at Elders to organise passage for him.

Phil had been able to keep his epilepsy a secret. He hadn't had a fit in a long time and for some months he'd been feeling better. He'd spent the past year working on cattle properties around the district without incident. He wanted to drive road trains and one day manage a big property of his own, but as I sat with him I knew things would probably not turn out that way.

Rob came back into the kitchen and told Phil that he'd organised a bus ticket back to Alice Springs. He told me to run him back into Elliott tomorrow and said sorry to Phil, gave him his pay, shook his hand and walked out. The next morning we drove away from Murranji with Phil's swag rolling around the back of the Tojo, and a sad looking Phil sitting up front. I dropped him off at Mary's shop, checked on the bus arrival, and said goodbye. As I drove back to the station I thought about my throbbing knee, and about Phil. How different he was from the little jockey from Adelaide — Phil was friendly, quiet and thoughtful, and the little prick from Adelaide was fit as a fiddle and a total wanker. The nice guy with the good attitude had problems, and the annoying little bloke with the mouth had none.

When I got back to Murranji there was a helicopter parked between the main house and the workshop. It looked smaller than I expected a chopper to be, lighter. I remembered seeing choppers in movies about Vietnam, but I'd never seen a mustering chopper before.

CHAPTER 7

In The Air Up There

I was starting to know where I was supposed to be when the team was out mustering a paddock, and I was falling off less. There were times I even successfully chased a wayward calf or steer back into the mob, my stockwhip cracking with a satisfying 'snap.' Horse and rider working as a sharp team, and so far I hadn't stuffed up. However, I had witnessed some great stuff ups. Ringers fooling around, breaking things and sometimes breaking themselves.

One early morning in June all the ringers were milling around at the yards, saddled up and ready to go. Chris was characteristically slow. He was also predictably cracking sick jokes and generally fooling around. He said to Mal, 'Watch me do a Roy Rogers.'

'This should be good,' I thought.

Chris had saddled up his bay stockhorse a few minutes earlier and he'd tethered it to the rails on the other side of the yard. As the rest of them watched, Chris ran at his horse from behind, planning to leap frog into the saddle with a 'Yeeha!' and then wave to his adoring fans. The bay had different ideas. It was as though his horse, Amigo, had seen it all before, as though it knew what to expect. Given the tendency for most ringers to do stupid shit at the slightest excuse, I assumed that Amigo had probably seen this very trick attempted many times before. So just at the right moment, just as Chris had started his assent over Amigo's arse with his legs spread wide and his hands firmly planted on Amigo's rump, the horse kicked. Chris let out a muffled grunt, the horse stepped sideways, and Chris hit the dust with another moan.

A couple of hours dry retching and Chris was back to normal. He caught up with the other riders later that morning, some of whom were still grinning when they thought about the sight of the flying cowboy. For the rest of the season, whenever any of us spoke to Chris we used a high-pitched tone. Chris rode up to me, nodded and said nothing. 'How's your nuts?' I squeaked, grinning. 'Shut up,' Chris replied.

We were entering the second phase of the season. For the next few months we'd ride a long way from the homestead, far to the north, out past Paradise Bore towards '5-Ways,' at the top end of the property. Some days we rode all day to get to some far-off set of temporary yards. Mitch and some of the other ringers would arrive in the truck with a welder, a box of tools, a big esky full of food and all the camping gear. They'd patch up the yards and get the gates working properly. The cattle would come to the only really permanent sources of water — the water troughs — and the ringers would 'trap' them into holding paddocks, ready to be walked back to the station. On some occasions the boss would speed up the process with the help of choppers.

Everyone got organised early. The boss told the ringers where to ride and gave the chopper pilots the layout of the fence lines. The choppers buzzed back and forth way out in the paddock, pushing all the cattle they could find towards the yards. Small mobs were pushed together to form one big, fast-moving mob. Long lengths of hessian were tied to steel posts to form 'wing' fences to guide the cattle into the big catching yards, and the ringers took flanking positions as the cattle appeared out of the scrub. You could see the dust clouds before you heard anything.

The first day that I was part of a chopper muster the horses and ringers began to get restless as swirls of dust were spotted, and the soft sound of rushing hooves and chopper blades started to build. The choppers were dancing around at the back of the mob. They jumped and bucked at times and at other moments they did a delicate pirouette to change direction completely. The cattle kept coming. 'This is the way to empty a long paddock,' I thought. You sit around close to the yards and simply help them in.

At just the right moment the pilots turned their choppers back towards the dusty horizon and the cattle slowed to a walk, and ambled into the waiting arms of the flanking ringers. We closed the circle behind the mob and penned them easily into the big yard. No nonsense, smooth. Rob was happy, everyone was happy. Rob said, 'They're all yours Mal,' and drove away to talk with the pilots about the layout of the next paddock. We loaded two road trains that day. Then we set up camp and got a peaceful night's sleep under the stars.

A Robinson chopper coming in to land at the airstrip on Murranji Cattle Station, Northern Territory.

There were generally two types of chopper mustering pilots working in the Territory. Ex-stockmen who'd spent a lot of time working cattle on the ground on horseback before taking to the air, and the 'cowboy pilots' who were either city pilots trying to make a name for themselves or ex-Vietnam veterans with a wild streak. The ex-ringers were sometimes family members of station owners and had been sponsored to gain their pilot's license. They were usually cattle-smart, sensible and reliable. The other pilots had a slightly more relaxed style.

The pilots working on Murranji that year were good operators — they'd grown up in the outback. They knew how close they needed to be to get a mob moving and they knew when an old bull needed a little more persuasion.

They also knew their machines from tip to tail and what aerobatics they were capable of.

The second day was pretty uneventful until late in the afternoon when the choppers came back to camp. The pilots stepped out after the engines were shut down and they ambled over to the fire. 'Anyone up for a spin?' asked one of the pilots to the small group of ringers sitting around the campsite. Mal said 'Take Andy for a look around. He's never been up.' Ray reminded Mal that Rob didn't like joyriding in the choppers, but Mal was interested to see if I was going to be able to eat dinner after a quick ride in one of the noisy over-sized dragonflies.

The pilot looked over at me and said 'Come on Stretch, leave your hat and grab some clean underwear.' He strolled back to where his chopper quietly sat, and I followed. The chopper was a modified Robinson R22 and low to the ground. I doubled over to walk under the flimsy-looking blades and squeezed myself into the passenger seat which was laid back at an angle, and fitted snugly at my shoulders. I felt as though I was in a formula one racing car. It started. I looked over at the pilot and asked 'What do you want me to do?' he told me to buckle up, put the headphones on, keep my arms inside the vehicle at all times and let him know if I felt like losing my lunch all over his bright little helicopter.

The blades starting turning. Faster and faster. The engine was screaming. Dust started to swirl all around. The vibrations through my seat were disturbing. Then, 'Woosh!' We took off straight up, so light but so powerful, and I thought my stomach was going to come out my bum. Then we were travelling horizontally looking directly at the ground rushing only metres beneath us and next I was looking straight up into the clear blue sky. My stomach came out my mouth. Good thing I didn't have anything intelligent to say right at that moment so I sat there gripping the edge of the frame, making soft squeaking noises. We ducked and dived and turned this way then that, tight turns and then sudden quiet hovers, then spins. The pilot looked over at me. I was coping surprisingly well. I hadn't turned blue.

The pilot slowed the chopper and gently landed on the ground next to the other machine. The blades slowed and the engine stopped. The pilot climbed out and went to see what was on for dinner but I sat there for a little while, contemplating the same thing. 'Soon,' I said to myself.

I wondered how they did that every day. Buzzing around, moving cattle, missing trees. I climbed out gingerly and walked slowly over to the campfire. Mal asked me from the other side of the camp if I felt like some stew. 'Not yet, thanks.'

It was another noisy night around the fire, another clear night sky full of stars. The other ringers ate beef stew thick with vegies, and damper and a cup of billy tea. I managed a small slice of damper, and a cuppa. The ringers told stories about home, about girls, and about big plans when the season was over to spend all their money in Darwin or the Alice, or further south. Martin was normally quieter than the rest, but this evening he regaled everyone with the story of his big catch — a sailfish he'd landed while deep-sea fishing off Darwin, 'The biggest fish any of you bloody amateurs will ever see.' Walter's guitar was never far away (unlike the ringers' voices which were anything but close to the right tune), and Peter squeaked along on the harmonica, slightly out of time. Most of us spread our swags around the campfire like spokes of a wheel. Some rolled theirs out on the back of the truck and a couple further out away from the fire, in the dark.

Even though we were out the back of the station, in the middle of a wide-open plain on the edge of the desert, it was not quiet at night. Insects constantly buzzed around, eager to get through any open folds in the mozzie nets that were thrown over the open ends of the ringers' swags. There was the occasional dingo howl, birds chattered away in nearby trees, and cows bawled for calves that had wandered off in the dark. And ringers were not the most silent of sleepers, especially if the cook had put a little too much garlic or Worcestershire Sauce in the stew. Stomachs rumbled and the wind blew.

I lay in my swag and gazed skywards, listening to the sounds, feeling as peaceful as a man can get. I wanted to do this forever, but I wondered if loneliness would come, if I'd miss my friends and family back home. The next morning I asked one of the chopper pilots if he enjoyed hopping from station to station, working away for months at a time. The pilot said, 'Look around, this is my home. And I've always got somewhere to go, somewhere different to check out. Who would want to be stuck in an office doing the same crap every day?'

I considered that for a while that night. One man's office job was another man's cattle muster. One man's contract was another's house to build. I had met men who worked on prawn trawlers and they said the same thing. They loved it. Ginger-growers in Gympie, the ferry operator in Cairns, and the publican in Mackay, they all seemed content with their thing. I was looking forward to another day doing my thing — another day in the saddle. As I lay in my swag a full moon rose over the desert horizon glowing bright orange and huge. It came up through the scrub to the east and lit up the landscape. I wished at that moment my Pop was there to enjoy it with me, and to be able to reminisce about it later.

The next day was spent working around 5-Ways Bore. The choppers brought another mob of cattle in and we drafted and tailed them to get them ready for the dusty walk back to the homestead. Everything was working smoothly — men, cattle and horses. Then one of the pilots stuffed up. It was mid-afternoon, really hot, really dusty. The choppers buzzed another mob in, but one of the pilots kept pushing. He just kept coming.

Mal was frantically waving his arms trying to get the chopper to 'Let go!' We could see what was about to happen, and there was nothing anyone could do about it. The mob came rushing in, and we could only watch as three hundred cattle stormed over the hessian wing, around the side of the yards and out into the paddock on the other side.

We galloped around the yards, flanking the rushing mob in a wide arc. We wheeled them slowly back to finally settle into a loose mob about a kilometre away. It took the rest of the day to get all the stragglers back, repair the yards and pen them for the night. Big John was lathered white and breathing heavily, and we were all pretty sore, exhausted and spent, but exhilarated at the same time. Even Chris was quieter than usual, no wisecracks or sick jokes all evening. Rob had settled down, the veins on his neck had stopped pulsating and he'd regained the tan colour in his cheeks. There wasn't as much singing or story-telling that evening, and the camp was full of the sound of snoring much earlier than usual.

Not long after the sun came up the next morning we organised the horses, had a quick smoko and then started the cattle out of the yards for the long walk home. By the next evening we were all settled back in the workmen's quarters, the horses were grazing down the front paddock, and there were more than two thousand cattle spread around the homestead paddock ready to get the Murranji special treatment. That would begin the next day but my first task was to head into town to meet another Murranji recruit, Henry, who'd travelled up from western New South Wales. He was looking for work to put money in his pocket so he could keep travelling across the Top End. He had a red Ford ute and an ugly black dog. I picked up the supplies from the store and said goodbye to Ron as I drove back to Murranji, Henry following in his ute. We pulled up at the yards just as Chris was saddling one of the spare horses, 'Thunder.'

'This should be good,' I thought as Henry and I wandered over to sit on the top rail and watch the action. Henry climbed up beside me and asked what was going on. 'Chris is just saddling one of the stockhorses for you,' I replied. 'We get two or three each. They're all pretty much the same, good cow horses.'

I had seen Thunder saddled once before, only once. Thunder was so girth proud that when you put a pad on him and pulled up the girth he'd buck and thrash about as if he was the baddest saddle bronc at the National Rodeo. Sure enough, Chris yanked on the cinch, found the hole for the buckle real quick and stood back. I watched Henry's face as he stared at the very large, very angry horse bucking and kicking as it farted and pig-rooted. Henry's eyes were wide as the horse fell over, got up, and bucked and farted again.

When Thunder finally settled down enough for Chris to lead him out into the bigger yard for a little 'reeducation,' Henry asked me quietly with a slight crack in his voice, 'Am I supposed to ride that?' 'No worries,' I replied, 'He's one of the quieter ones.' I introduced Henry to the others, left them talking about the horses and walked back to the Tojo.

Chris spent a lot of time with Thunder over the next week and he came good after a while. With a lot of attention from Chris and with help from Mal and Ray he turned into a pretty good cow horse. Chris said that sitting on Thunder was like sitting on a Ferrari on fast idle. He was always vibrating. He seemed ready to jump clear out of the saddle at the slightest opportunity. Henry never had to ride him, and he was glad about that. He was given two of the quieter horses and spent about four weeks on Murranji, lending a hand.

At Murranji there was about sixty horses, all types — big brown geldings, bay mares and small chestnut stockhorses, old and young. There was a pretty little buckskin mare and a huge dark horse with an ugly head. There were also a couple of little grey ponies that thought themselves pretty handy as well. They seemed positively disappointed the mornings that they got run in with the mob of working horses but didn't get picked out for a day's work mustering. Most of the horses were broken and most of them were used most of the time. They all had their own personalities, their own attitudes, but there was a dozen or so that had never been handled, let alone broken. For one unbroken little grey pony that was about to change.

'The handsome creamy mare in the roundyard fringed by stringybarks is wary, her ears back, her eyes watchful. She turns sharply in the soft dirt, darting left, then right, anything to avoid contact with the neatly bearded man leaning on the fence. His body, in sharp contrast, is relaxed; his jeaned legs are still, his steely blue eyes downcast beneath a buckskin hat.'

Outback Magazine,
Story By Amanda Burdon

CHAPTER 8
Horses For Causes

Mungo was a big man. He must have weighed twenty stone and he used to say, 'It's all muscle.' He could eat twelve Weet-Bix and a half a loaf of bread in one sitting. He could also put away enough cowboy casserole to feed three normal-sized men. Luckily he was also a nice fella. He was handy in the yards because when you needed to hold a young steer on the ground while someone cuts its nuts out, it was good having Mungo around. When he sat on you, you stayed down. And then there was his effect on the horses. When Mal had one with an attitude problem or needed 'reeducation' because it started dropping its head at inopportune times, you gave it to Mungo to ride for a few days.

Early in the season Mal had a go at a tough-looking little grey pony that ran with the big mob of horses in the front paddock, but he had no luck breaking it in to the bit. It possessed what Mal described as 'personality issues.' Then Mungo turned up and Mal started thinking about the tough little grey pony again. He introduced it to Mungo early one Sunday morning, and I wandered down to the yards to take a look.

Mal had already run the station horses into the yards so together we drafted off the grey. We ran it up the steel race and when it got to the head bale I shoved a steel post into the gate behind its legs to stop it backing out. Mal and I quietly put a breaking pad (a cheap old saddle used for breaking in rough horses), a rope halter and a breastplate on the horse, while Mungo climbed up onto the rails and straddled the steel rails above.

When Mal was done Mungo lowered himself down onto the grey, grabbed a handful of mane and got a tight grip on the reins. I could tell that the horse was feeling the extra pounds that just arrived, and it was starting to get worked up and breathing heavily. Then Mal swung the rail-gate wide and horse and rider turned outwards into the main yard.

The horse took two steps and then tried to buck. It arched its back and dropped its head, and let out a low grunt as it kicked out, but it had no joy. It looked like it was more worried about keeping upright on its four shaky legs, and it very soon gave up thinking about ejecting the big man on its back. Instead, it settled down with a simple case of the shakes. 'Bloody great,' said Mal, 'Worked a treat. I've got a couple of others I'd like you to take a look at, Mungo.'

'No worries bro,' said Mungo, as he walked the little horse around the boundary, steering it this way and that. Then he pulled up near where we were standing and leaned over to get off. He swung his offside leg back over the horse's rump in the usual way. However, just then the little grey horse took full advantage of the rider being off the side and unbalanced, and kicked out as hard and high as it could. There was a yell from Mungo as he was ejected, and then a grunt as he hit the dust. No time for laughs this time. Another ringer could probably tuck and roll, take a fall and bounce. But not Mungo. When he fell he went 'thud,' and it took both of us to help him into the Tojo and run him back to the workmen's quarters. He complained the whole way and promised Mal a punch in the head if he ever got the notion to ask for a repeat performance of that day's antics.

This was a pity indeed for Mal because the 'Mungo treatment' worked so well on the grey. After some more special attention it earned the name 'Dime' because of its ability to slide to a stop and turn around on one. And it turned into a handy little cow pony. For a short horse it was really tough, and would trot all day in the heat and dust following a mob of cattle, and nudging the little calves along at the tail. Mal experimented later that month with a similar idea on a similarly untrained horse with a similar bad attitude to the grey. He put two ringers up in the breaking pad at once. He expected the weight of two ringers to have the same affect as one Mungo, but the results were not pretty, especially for the young fella who got a clean hoof to the head and a black eye for a week. Mal stopped experimenting after that and went back to the good old ways — working a green horse for hours in the round yard, the long reins, the weeks of slow, methodical, routine work.

First, you get the horse quiet, get it used to being handled. Then you introduce it to a bridle, a bit, and the long reins. Next you tie on a pad and a girth, then bag it down softly by flapping an old saddle blanket onto its legs and its flanks. Then get on, and hold on. Mal seemed to know when it was just the right time to throw his leg over. He took his time, and did it right. One evening in the kitchen when all the ringers were swapping advice about the best way to break horses, with me and the other jackaroos listening intently, Ray said breaking a horse was like loving a woman, 'You start slow and easy, but then you show them who's boss.' Martin laughed and said, 'What would you know old man, you couldn't break a sweat.' Ray simply continued as if the bugger had never spoken, 'You earn their trust, you talk softly to them, then you jump on and hang on tight.' Later on in a more serious moment Ray said to me, 'Never over-break 'em. You don't want nothin' left. You still want it to want to work hard for you.'

Then there was the way Garry used to do it. He said he loved riding buck-jumpers, 'The nastier the better.' Garry's horses were never fully broken, and he liked it that way, they never shook him. Garry talked about the wild horse he was breaking in the main yards that first day when I arrived at the station. He simply ran it up the race, saddled it and rode it bucking into the main yard until it settled down. The two horses Garry used when everyone went out on a big muster, 'Mad Jack' and 'Cujo,' were horses like that. Nasty types compared to the others. On one outback muster, when we were all breaking camp and saddling up Garry chucked his saddle on Mad Jack, ripped the girth up and jumped on. He came bucking and yelling through the camp, spooking the others and disturbing the peace. 'Look Out!' he yelled as he thundered through, then took a long wide arc out into the paddock and came bucking back through the camp, laughing and yelling and enjoying the hell out of it all.

One day at full gallop chasing a steer back into a mob he came off, and came off bad. This surprised everyone because he'd done the same thing a thousand times before without a problem. We thought he was invincible, but this day was different. Garry and a bunch of other ringers were back at the station working skittish cattle in the front paddock. The mob they were tailing had spent most of the year lazing around in the far-off long paddocks before a bunch of strangers came along and bundled them into tight pens in big trucks, and dumped them in a strange part of the country.

So it was that Garry found himself busier than usual that afternoon. All the cattle wanted to do was bolt towards the scrub and trees to the north of the homestead. It was a hot day, and everyone was feeling it. You could see the haze drifting up like morning steam off the dam. The earth was dry, and deep cracks criss-crossed all over the ground. In the wet season the black soil was sticky and you couldn't drive through most of the paddocks because the mud quickly packed up on your tyres and you'd just sit there and spin, but in the dry, which was most of the year, the ground was hard and cracked like big chunks of concrete.

Garry was coming around hard, leaning way out of the saddle at full gallop and cracking his stockwhip on a wayward steer's arse when Mad Jack's front hoof went into a deep hole. They both went over and slid and tumbled. Garry stopped sliding and tumbling before Mad Jack who tumbled right over him. It wasn't pretty. I could tell it was a hard fall because Garry wasn't moving as his horse stumbled to its feet and shook itself violently. His arm wasn't sitting right and bent too far backwards around his neck. As he lay broken on the hard ground one of the jackaroos raced to the yards to find Rob, and the rest of us galloped over to where Garry had fallen. Dave was the first one there and was off his horse before it stopped. I watched him bend down and put his ear close to Garry's face, then lift his head and swing his arm back around to his side where it was supposed to be. As I rode up it seemed as if Garry had come to. He was swaying his head back and forth on Dave's arm and flailing about with his good arm. He groaned as blood started streaming down his face.

It suddenly struck me exactly where I was. Standing there holding the reins of my horse, looking down at Garry while Dave and the other riders talked about the best thing to do. I remembered I couldn't ring a taxi or jump in my car and drive to the nearest emergency department. When bad things happen out there you know that professional help is far away. 'Hand me your belt,' said Dave, which brought me back, and I handed my belt to him and he strapped it around Garry's neck as a sling. He wiped down his face and held his bloody handkerchief to the cut over Garry's eye. One of the others donated his shirt and Dave tied it around Garry's head as a turban to stop the flow.

Garry stopped groaning loudly, but his arm and shoulder must have been really hurting because he was drifting in and out and breathing deeply. Rob turned up with Ray and they checked Garry over before they bundled him into the back and drove slowly back to the homestead. Rob was up on the tray, leaning back against the cabin, cradling Garry in his arms.

We went back to tailing the mob, cautiously then, and we saw the plane coming in low over the main yards later that afternoon. It made a wide circle around the homestead, buzzed the cattle off the airstrip and came around for a second attempt at landing. It glided softly down the runway and taxied over to stop at the back of the workshop. It was one of the planes operating the Northern Territory Flying Doctor Service and had flown in to pick up Garry for the trip to Alice Springs Base Hospital for x-rays. Rob bandaged Garry up like an expert, and they gave him more painkillers and put him on the plane. Ray told the ringers later that evening around the kitchen table that Rob had seen his fair share of breaks, blood and bruises in his time. He reckoned that the boss was better qualified than most of the real doctors he'd met. 'Years of first-hand experience.' I found out later it was a long flight for Garry that day. They'd two other stops to make before they got to the Alice — a sick baby in Tennant Creek, and a grandfather with chest pains. Garry never came back to Murranji that season. He'd busted his shoulder and his knee, and his black curly head had been opened up with a deep cut above his right eye. His head came good pretty quickly but his shoulder was never the same.

I ran into Garry back in Elliott later that year while on a perishables run and he asked me about his horses. I could tell he wanted to get back out there, get back on. I couldn't imagine what it was like, never able to chase cattle or ride buck-jumpers again. I once again thought about my grandfather: 'Your life can change direction in a heartbeat,' he'd say. 'You think everything is normal when you wake up, but by lunchtime you're swingin' in the breeze again.'

'Why do doctors slap babies' butts right after they're born? To knock the penises off the smart ones.'

Anonymous

CHAPTER 9
Run Away Tractor

Mitch the mechanic was not happy. He was working on one of the bore pumps and it wasn't cooperating. He was yelling and throwing tools. He often threw tools around the workshop when he got frustrated, and mechanicing was a frustrating job. The bore pump was an old Lister diesel, and it refused to start. Lister diesels were relatively simple machines. They're a pretty standard hand-cranked affair with a cast iron body and only a small number of simple moving parts. No complicated electrics and no spark required. The combustion chamber held such great compression that when you introduced a fine mist of atomised diesel through the injector lines as you gave it a good heave on the crank, it'd start up and tick over for as long as it had diesel in the tank. During quiet times around Murranji two of us would drive around the bores, refilling the big diesel tanks and re-starting the pumps. But every so often, like this day, a pump would decide not to cooperate.

Mitch took the bloody thing apart three times. He tested everything individually and put it all back together. But nothing. No joy to be had. Added to that, the fact was that whenever you wanted to start a diesel bore pump you had to grab the shiny black crank handle and heave with all your might, to overcome the high compression. It became very frustrating very fast if it didn't fire up the first couple of cranks.

Mitch spent four hours working on the unhelpful machine and hadn't once got that satisfying 'phhhht phhhhht' sound that signified diesel was getting fed properly, and it was about to fire up. I heard another spanner hit the tin wall of the workshop, and another 'Bloody Hell!' as I was greasing saddles in the nearby tack room with Dave. We decided to wander over and check on Mitch. We thought we could probably stand around and be totally useless and ask stupid questions, thus giving the mechanic much needed support by providing a couple of new targets.

Dave and I got about halfway across to the workshop when Mitch came running out with what looked like a large piece of diesel bore pump held above his head. He chucked it as hard as he could in the general direction of the dam where it hit the dirt and bounced twice. He looked up as we walked over and said, 'Bring that bloody thing back in here and I'll cut it up with the oxy,' and stormed back into the workshop. A couple of minutes later Mitch came around from behind the workshop in one of the old station four-wheel-drives and yelled at Dave and I to jump in. 'Let's go get that bloody tractor out from below the dam.'

One of the young jackaroos had bogged the old Ford a few weeks earlier. He'd got it stuck while digging a trench to lay poly-pipe from the dam to a new horse trough in the front paddock. While looking backwards at the trench he drove straight into a bog hole. The tractor was in low gear with its accelerator stuck on. Thick black mud built up quickly under the guards and the tractor went down to its axles.

Three weeks later I was knee-deep in thick black mud trying to dig the tractor out of its trench. Dave was helping dig, and Mitch was trying to get it started again. With some coaxing it fired up in big black clouds of diesel smoke and Mitch lifted the trench-digger out of the mud. He disconnected the implement from the back of the tractor, locked the diffs, and had a go at driving it out of the bog. The wheels simply spun in the mud. 'Time for plan B,' Mitch said to us as he shut it down, jumped off and walked confidently towards the truck.

He turned it around and backed up to the tractor, grabbed a steel tow cable from out of the back, hooked it to the tow bar and walked the other end over to the front of the tractor. He looped it around the front axle and got Dave to jump in the truck while he climbed onto the tractor and started her up again. Then he yelled 'let her rip!' to Dave and gunned the tractor once more. Engines revved, wheels spun, the cable snapped tight, but there was no forward movement. Then Mitch got another bright idea. Looking back it was a pretty stupid idea, but it shone brightly nonetheless. He thought he'd leave the tractor in gear, with the accelerator stuck on, and the wheels turning in the mud. Then he'd jump off, grab me, and go and pick up a heavy log lying just over the other side of the bog to use as a lever to lift the tractor out of the mud. He yelled at me to help him in his quest.

Anyone looking on could quickly surmise that for three normally handy station hands there wasn't half a brain between us at that moment. Dave was revving his engine, spinning the wheels, and the cable was dancing up and down between the truck and the tractor as the truck skidded and bucked on the dry ground. The tractor was blowing black smoke skyward as it sat there slowly spinning in the wet mud, with Mitch and I over the other side of the bog, tugging at an old fence post that was half stuck in the mud.

Yep, then it happened...

Dave gunned his engine one more time and the tractor came loose. Mitch and I looked up and instantly realised our folly. Dave looked in his rear view mirror and wondered briefly why there was nobody at the steering wheel of the tractor — as it lunged in his direction. He looked over his shoulder to check that he wasn't seeing things in the mirror and then turned the steering wheel slightly to the left to let the tractor overtake him slowly on his right.

As Mitch and I were squelching furiously through the mud we looked up and realised what was going to happen. The tractor was moving pretty quickly now. Unencumbered from the digger and the bog hole it took off as though it was a stockhorse headed home after a big day out. It ran over the cable that was dragging along behind Dave and then powered on past. Dave bailed out a couple of seconds later. He simply stopped the truck, got out and ran in the opposite direction. For some reason only he knows how to explain, he yanked the handbrake on before he got out, so the truck stopped, and the tractor drove on. It had the wind in its nostrils now and freedom in its sights. Mitch and I made it to dry ground and started running in the direction of all the action as the cable once again went tight, only this time the opposite way around.

The tractor's pace now slowed and it pulled the station truck around sideways, then over onto its side with a crash. The cable came loose and the tractor took off once again. It wasn't really moving that fast but it was fast enough to give two mud-covered men a run for their money. It was one of those times when you really needed someone with a hand-held video camera to catch all the action. But it probably wasn't something the three of us would've liked to revisit later in Technicolor.

I was the fastest of the three. My legs pounded over the ground as bits of mud flew off my jeans and my hat flew off dramatically behind me. I caught up with the tractor after about fifty yards and then in a moment of clarity I had a thought. 'What the hell am I gonna do now?' The tractor's big gnarly-looking tyres were spinning and bucking on the uneven ground, and the steering wheel was slowly turning left and right as if the old Ford didn't want to get caught.

I took a look around as I ran, and scanned the horizon in front. There were about eighty kilometres of Murranji paddocks between the tractor and Lake Woods, with only three fence lines in-between. I considered letting go the chase and simply wandering back to the homestead to organise some fencing gear, but I decided to try something. I thought the safest place to be (if there was anything 'safe' about what I was about to try) was behind the tractor, rather than running alongside and trying to reach in-between the big spinning wheels. As I ran around behind and reached out for one of the arms on the three-point linkage I stumbled over a crack in the dirt and hit the ground with a thud. I stood up, dusted myself off and gave up the chase.

Then Mitch ran past. He slapped me on the shoulder as he ran and yelled with glee, 'Come on old mate!' Mitch was enjoying himself. In a weird way it was like a release of tension from the morning's episode with the stubborn bore pump. We ran. We laughed and we ran. Another fifty yards and we caught up with the tractor. I reached out from behind again and got a good hold of the top link. I jumped up onto the tow bar, then pulled myself up and over the back of the driver's seat, pushed the clutch in, knocked it into neutral and slammed on the brakes with a loud, 'Woohoo!'

Dave was waiting back at the overturned four-wheel-drive, quietly making another rollie as Mitch and I pulled up on the tractor. We used the tow cable to pull the four-wheel-drive back onto its wheels and drove back to the workshop from where the fun had started. We bashed the tow bar back straight, cleaned the mud off the tractor and laughed about what happened.

Then Mitch looked up and shielded his eyes from the glare as he stared across the front paddocks to the track that led from Elliott to the southeast. 'Look what's coming,' he said.

You couldn't sneak into Murranji during the daytime. The dust cloud rising from your vehicle signalled your arrival from miles away. But the dust cloud we were watching that day was different. It was smaller than a truck, and moving faster. It was a motorcycle, coming fast. It took about ten minutes from the time we spotted the dust to when the bike came blasting into the compound and straight over to the workmen's quarters, as though the rider knew exactly where he was going.

The three of us walked out of the workshop, one of us making a rollie and one cleaning a greasy engine part with an old rag. The third one, me, stopped dead in his tracks as the motorcycle rider dismounted, ripped off <u>her</u> helmet and shook out a long bushy mane of dark wavy hair. Female, very female. 'Bloody Hell! This is not good,' said Mitch, 'Not good at all.' Dave made an agreeable grunt to acknowledge Mitch's observation as he walked away and tried to look busy. Mitch took one last look and walked back into the workshop, muttering something about hoping Rob decides to hold back the grog this weekend.

I wondered what weekend grog had to do with the arrival of a female biker at the station? It only took a couple of days before I found out. All the ringers at Murranji look forward to Saturday night for two reasons. No work the next morning, and the keys to the grog safe. As head stockman, Mal was in charge of the grog ration. Rob gave him the keys on Saturday around mid-afternoon and Mal returned them on Sunday morning. All the ringers and jackaroos were allowed one six-pack each, and they only had one choice to make that year on Murranji — 'green cans' (Vic Bitter) or 'red cans' (Melbourne Bitter). I never found out why it was that Murranji ringers in the middle of the Northern Territory were drinking Victorian brew when there was perfectly good Top End beers like Emu brand available.

Dave couldn't handle his grog. He only needed four cans before he fell apart. On some Saturday nights he was really friendly after four beers, and he wanted to hug everyone and tell them they were his best mates ever. On others he wanted to fight anyone who looked at him sideways. Chris was a 'red can man.' He used to say that it tasted like mother's milk. The effect, however, was quite different. If he was thirsty he'd drink his six beers really quickly, and then lie down somewhere, anywhere, and mumble quietly as he slept. Then again, the similarities seem obvious.

Mungo decided long ago never to drink alcohol, Mitch only ever drank one or two, and Ray was pretty happy after he downed a couple of green cans. Martin on the other hand used to hang out for Saturday night. During the week he was quiet and surly, but for an hour or two on a Saturday evening after the grog was handed around he was nearly friendly. But after he downed his fourth can he became nasty. If nobody wanted to fight him he liked to break things, and throw things, and yell obscenities until well past midnight. On one Saturday evening he was cunning enough to sneak the keys to the grog safe from Mal's belt and pinch a couple of cases of red cans for himself. Maybe at one time in his life he was a happy young fella but now he was just an angry drunk. And his girlfriend had just turned up on a shiny Honda motorcycle.

CHAPTER 10

Grog and Women

She said 'hey' as she untied her bag from the back of the motorcycle, took her jacket off and hung it over the seat. I replied with a similarly casual 'hey' as I sauntered over to greet this interesting new arrival. She was all woman, bumps and grooves in all the right places, a faded tattoo on her bare shoulder and a shiny little belly ring that jingled as she moved — and she loved me. The way she looked up at me, the way she leaned forward and blinked her eyelids as she reached out to shake my hand. She seemed breathless, she could hardly say hello. Poor girl. She must have fallen for me right then and there. She'd never be the same again.

I was about to launch into witty conversation. To recount a litany of interesting anecdotes about exciting times and impressive stories about dangers overcome. But she walked away. She wandered off towards the kitchen, leaving me standing there with a dopey grin on my face and staring blankly at the bum squirming inside her tight jeans. As I walked back towards the workshop I thought how the girl seemed so out of place in the compound at Murranji. So different, so fresh.

For months I'd lived and worked with a bunch of hairy, smelly and often times rough men. Except for the wives down at the blackfella's camp, and Rob's wife who brought meals to the workmen, and could sometimes be seen dressed in sensible shirts and baggy trousers hanging washing out the back of the big house, there wasn't a lot of soft female-type action on the station. The presence of the gold and chrome motorcycle in the compound added to the strangeness of the apparition.

As Mitch and I gave the Ford tractor a service, Mitch kept complaining about the girl's arrival. He'd seen it happen before. He told me a story about another property where a bunch of ringers were mustering and fencing — normal days followed by normal nights — but then a girl appeared and within three days they all hated each other. 'It's like springtime in the paddocks,' he said seriously, 'The bloody bulls start fighting over the young heifers and there's trouble every day.' I couldn't understand. 'We just need to be sensible,' I said to Mitch, who answered with a wave of his spanner. 'You watch what bloody happens around here now my boy.'

It wasn't very long before I saw Mitch's prediction come true as Martin threw Mal through the screen door of the kitchen. 'Keep your bloody hands off my girlfriend!' yelled Martin as he shoved him with his boot. Sure enough Mal was the head stockman at Murranji, and all the ringers respected him, but he shouldn't have flicked her on the arse like that. Maybe he was looking for trouble. 'He's normally such a sensible bloke' Chris said to Mungo, who replied with a disapproving grunt.

It was Saturday night and we'd all had more than our allocated share of grog. Things were starting to get a bit loose around Murranji, and Rob noticed it too. The ringers were preoccupied, distracted most of the time, and Rob found us harder to start in the mornings. Then one day, as he drove into the homestead around lunchtime he noticed the girl sun-baking on the lawn out the front of the workmen's quarters. 'Yep,' he thought as he drove over to the workshop, 'There's the problem.' He pulled up at the front of the workshop and said to Mitch through his window, 'That explains why them buggers are so keen to mow lawns and plant trees around the homestead and help you in the workshop all of a sudden.'

'I tried to tell the other fellas, but they weren't bloody listening,' Mitch told him. 'There's no room for females in a herd of horny bulls when it 'aint bloody joining time,' he said as he craned his head around the truck to get another look.

She left the next day, and so did Martin. They strapped what they could onto her motorcycle and took off early in the morning. Rob was going to post the rest of Martin's gear to an address in Alice Springs. 'There's no room for a trouble-makin' girl around here,' he told Martin as he paid him out and showed them the front gate.

The ringers returned to normal soon after the pair had left. Well, as close to 'normal' as ringers can get. It was late June when daytime temperatures can touch forty degrees, but the nights were still cool. Mornings were the most pleasant time of day, except for one Sunday morning when I woke with a shotgun up my nose. I was in the middle of a pleasant dream about pretty girls in bikinis when I felt cold steel touching my face, then ramming up my nose, the barrels cold, shiny, and hard. My mind was foggy — it was always a bit foggy until about ten o'clock in the morning. 'Holy shit,' I squeaked out.

If I tried to grab the gun, would the shooter slip a finger? I was looking up the barrels at the two flimsy-looking firing pins at the other end. I thought how close I was to death, again, and it really started to hurt. Hard steel being shoved onto soft tissue and cartilage. The bastard holding the shotgun was 'Bob,' a buffalo shooter from Queensland, and the other was 'Stu' from Perth. They'd been travelling around the Top End together, working on different stations with no real plan or direction. They'd arrived at Murranji earlier that week and had been pissed for most of the time. Rob didn't know they had a huge esky full of beer in the back of the Toyota they were driving.

The two men laughed and snorted as they stood over me in my cot. They were still pretty pissed. I strangely wondered what time it was, the sun wasn't even close to coming up yet. Luckily the gun didn't go off. Bob gave it one last shove at my face then lifted it up and threw it over his shoulder. He laughed loudly as he grabbed his mate around the neck and staggered towards the door to see what other trouble they could cause. I wanted to jump up and smash them with something, grab the old steel camp chair from beside the door and smash them both over the back of the head with it. But I didn't. I lay in bed, relieved that I was still alive but pissed off just the same. It could have been really bad. 'Bastards!'

I was up early that morning. I walked quietly past the screen door on Bob's room and could hear his loud snoring. A raspy wheeze came from Stu in his cot across the room. I made myself a coffee in the kitchen and settled down to wait. Some of the other jackaroos came in, scratching their heads and rubbing their faces as they slowly woke up. Twenty minutes later and all the workmen were up and ready to go, except for the two newcomers, the buffalo shooter and his mate, still snoring loudly.

Then the boss turned up. By this stage in the season Rob didn't have to go down the line of rooms in the workmen's quarters and slam on screen doors and yell 'Come on!' to get us moving in the morning. We were normally ready to go when we heard the soft squeak of the brakes on the boss's Tojo as it pulled up out front. We'd already had a cuppa and some cereal or toast, and were ready to go before the sun.

Everyone filed out of the kitchen and walked across the lawn to climb up onto the back of Rob's truck. Mal said to Rob that he was going to rustle-up the two new blokes, and ran off towards Bob's room. Ray jumped up beside Rob in the front and the ringers climbed up onto the back, all except me. I waited on the grass, about halfway between the tuck and the quarters.

We could hear Mal slam the screen door as he went into Bob and Stu's room to kick the two of them awake and get them moving. 'Come on you slack bastards!' he yelled, 'Everyone's waiting.' Thirty seconds later and Mal came out of the room with two very sleepy, disheveled-looking men stumbling behind him trying to pull their boots on. They were both still wearing the dusty jeans and shirts they'd worn the day before, so a hat and boots was all they needed to get ready for work. To be fully functional they probably could have done with a cuppa and some breakfast, but that was not to be. 'Get up here Andy,' called Chris from the back of the Tojo, but I didn't move. I stood there facing the quarters with my feet firmly planted. Mal raised an eyebrow to me in question as he walked past. I shifted my weight to my other foot.

Bob had his boots on by this time and he was moving a bit faster. But he was still very foggy and he hardly noticed me standing in front of him. Just as Bob went to walk around me, just at the right moment, I put my left leg across in front of the buffalo shooter, planted my foot firmly on the ground and gave him a shove between the shoulder blades. Bob was not ready for it and he hit the ground on his side with a thud. 'You've gotta be more careful,' I said, 'You could hurt yourself tripping over like that.'

'What the fuck?' said Bob menacingly as he got to his feet and squared up to me. The ringers looked on but no one said anything. 'You,' I said, 'You're the fuckwit.' Bob swung his right fist in a predictably wide arc at my chin and I thought briefly that it might have seemed a little unfair to the onlookers that I was wide-awake, fully rested, and not hung over, while my opponent was shaky after a late night on the grog. But the thought quickly passed, like Bob's right arm as it swung harmlessly over the top of my head as I ducked out of the way. I threw a short jab to Bob's ear and pinged him nicely on target. Then I followed with a straight right-hander to the chin that connected with a satisfying 'crack' and Bob's head snapped backwards. Bob fell over, again, just as Stu came to life.

Stu had no idea why this tall fella was smacking his friend around but he suddenly thought he should do something about it, so he lunged at me. 'Hold It!' yelled Rob as he jumped out of the Tojo, but Stu kept coming. He bunched his pudgy hand into a fist as he lunged, but I was ready. I repeated the maneuver I'd used on Bob and Stu hit the ground beside his mate.

I said to Bob as he groggily got to his feet, 'That's for sticking your bloody shotgun up my nose last night you bastard.' Then I added, 'You want some more slapping?' Bob looked like he was about to try and have another go but the boss got there just in time to put his body between the two of us. He told me to get onto the truck, and he told Bob and Stu to get into the kitchen. 'I'll come back and deal with you two idiots after I get this lot down to the yards,' he said as he stomped back to the driver's side of the truck.

I rubbed my knuckles as we drove down to the yards to start the day properly. Nobody on the back said anything, or asked any questions — there'd be time enough to talk about it later on. Rob dropped us off at the main yards, gave us orders for the day and drove back to the homestead. Around nine that morning the two latest Murranji visitors drove off down the track, headed for town. They'd been given their marching orders, packed their truck and been let out.

'I don't want any of that sort of trouble around here,' Rob told them as he handed over their cheques. He meant 'grog trouble.' That's why he kept it locked up and used to say that station managers always had trouble on 'wet' stations. 'Staying dry is the best way to go.' Later that afternoon when we were sitting around the branding fire talking about the early morning events, Rob said to the men, 'Women and grog are real trouble, especially when you combine the two.' Well the next couple of months were going to be relatively stress-free for Rob because the ringers were about to enter into a long period without either.

'...the drought will go on drying while there's anything to dry, then it rains until you'd fancy it would bleach the sunny sky —Then it pelters out of reason, for the downpour day and night, nearly sweeps the population to the Great Australian Bight.'

The City Bushman,
Henry Lawson 1892

CHAPTER 11
FAR OUT BACK

One evening Mal and Ray and the others sat around the kitchen table and told stories of riding the far corners of other Northern Territory cattle properties and coming on to cleanskin 'mickey' bulls so big and arrogant they'd chase a horse and rider. The sight of a seven hundred kilo bull with long angry-looking pointy horns blasting out of the scrub would put the wind up any outback rider. Chris told a remarkable story about a particularly cagey mickey bull that he'd met near Katherine — a story that was both hard to believe and impossible to prove, but thrillng nonetheless. He said it shifted itself around behind a tree so that all he could see was the pointy ends of its horns poking out from both sides as he rode by. Mungo told him to save his bullshit bedtime stories for travelling tourists as he held him down and made him eat teabags and threatened to cut off his sideburns with his pocketknife.

Murranji belonged to Rob's family. They owned five properties around the region, all managed by other family members, and they operated a fleet of road trains that could transport cattle between stations to areas that had good feed and water supplies. Murranji was one link in this chain of stations.

Murranji was like other cattle stations in the Northern Territory, so big you couldn't muster all the stock by chasing them around on horseback. There are three ways that cattle are collected up there. The first involves ringers mustering mobs relatively close to the homestead to work them in the main yards. These are mostly day trips and the ringers are never too far from their quarters, the kitchen and a home-cooked meal. The second, and by far the most practiced, is by 'trapping' them to water. The ringers travel out to stock camps at far-off bores on the property, to areas in the north such as 'Buchanan,' and trap cattle to fenced-off water troughs for weeks at a time. Rob used to say that controlling the water was the key. Cattle will walk many kilometres on well-trodden tracks in such dry and dense scrubby country to be gathered up by waiting ringers. The third way is with the help of choppers that push the cattle to waiting riders at portable yards, which are then driven back to the homestead on horseback, or loaded straight onto road trains for the trip to market.

The yards at Buchanan (named after 'Bluey' Buchanon who pioneered the Murranji Track in 1886) consisted of two very large yards — a trapping yard and a holding yard. There was also a smaller drafting yard, a race and a loading ramp at the site. Thirsty cattle came in to the first big yard to drink at the trough and every couple of hours one of the ringers quietly rode down to the big yard, closed the gate, then pushed them through to the holding yard. The ringer then opened the gate to the trapping yard again. It was simple, quiet and efficient. Ringers normally trapped in pairs. One rode down to the trapping yard to push cattle through, and the other tended the camp or cooked a meal or got some sleep. Then they'd swap.

Most ringers enjoyed trapping season. The camping was easy and there were no real chores to speak of. Chris loved it because you didn't have to try and look busy in case the boss was lurking, and the only worries you had were packs of dingoes, the odd deadly snake, scorpions in your swag, and the occasional mickey bull. Trapping sounded like boys' own adventures the way Mal and the others talked, and I was getting wound up just thinking about it. Rob had dinner in the kitchen in the workmen's quarters with us one evening leading up to it. He'd spent a lot of his young working life with gangs of ringers who were responsible for trapping and mustering and droving at outlying paddocks on various properties, and he spoke of his love of that time.

In the second week of July, Chris and I headed for the northernmost trapping camp on Murranji, 'Buchanan Downs.' We had two horses in the horse float and all our gear on the back of the four-wheel-drive. Ray and Mitch had left earlier that day with a truckload of supplies, fencing tools and camping gear. They'd get to Buchanan Downs first, set up camp and then check the yards, water troughs and the bore pump that fed water into the turkey's nest dam. Chris and I were going to meet them there with the horses and then settle in for about four weeks.

Rob turned up every three days or so with an esky full of corned beef, a box of supplies consisting of flour, spuds, greens, cans of tinned soup, coffee, tea and a couple of bottles of the outback ringer's friend, Worcestershire Sauce — everything a couple of hungry ringers needed to survive. Mitch or one of the other ringers came up at the end of every week with a truckload of hay for the horses and for the cattle resting quietly in the holding yards. Mitch sometimes smuggled a couple of six-packs of green cans from the Saturday night stash, and Chris sunk them into the cool water of the dam for later.

We took it in turns to cook over the fire pit in the big black, well-used camp oven. I enjoyed cooking damper. It was satisfying getting everything right — the mixture, the amount of bi-carb and salt, the temperature of the coals from the fire that were placed on the lid, and the length of time I left it cooking in the hole next to the campfire. Most mornings we organised a good breakfast of damper, corned beef warmed up in a frypan, tinned soup and a coffee. Dinner was normally damper, corned beef, some greens, tinned soup and a cup of tea. We achieved a small amount of variety by either having the damper drenched or undrenched in the savory-tasting Worcestershire Sauce.

The most important piece of equipment at Buchanan Downs was the Lister diesel bore pump. This pulled ground-water from deep under the dusty plain and pumped it up into the man-made turkey's nest dam to fill the cattle troughs, and two thirsty ringers. Every couple of hours one of us rode down to the bore and refilled the plastic fuel tank hanging from the old windmill stand above the pump. Then we'd spin the big crank handle to get the pump going again. We quickly got used to the quiet 'phhhht phhhht' sound that drifted up to camp from where the pump tirelessly chugged away.

The turkey's nest dam was a really practical way to store water. It was a donut-shaped circle of earth and clay pushed up by a bulldozer. The dam was then filled from the bore pump over time through a long piece of four-inch plastic poly-pipe running from the pump under the old windmill stand. The water coming out of the ground tasted of salt and minerals, but after a time in the dam it would settle out and become fit to drink.

We had a number of choices for staying clean. The water coming out of the bore pump travelled hundreds of metres over the sun-baked ground, so by the time it got to the dam and shot out of the poly pipe six feet above the water level it was hot. During the middle of the day it was a hot shower, better than back at the workmen's quarters. We could jump in the dam for a cool swim, or opt for a hot bath in one of the cattle troughs. All we had to do was block the float valve with a big rock, move away to the trees and let the cattle drink the trough dry. Then we could wander back, take the rock out from the valve and the hot water coming through the poly pipe across the same hot ground would refill the trough. Add one ringer and a cake of Palmolive Gold, and you had five-star ablutions.

Conversation around the campsite was light. We could go for a whole day and only say ten words. We knew what we had to do and we did it without much fuss. Chores were carried out in regular harmony with only the occasional bit of excitement — like when the mickey bull came through camp. I was returning with an armload of firewood when I heard Chris cursing and yelling. I ran the last hundred metres and appeared just in time to see the animal pushing one of the eskies around in the dust with its huge head. For half an hour we threw sticks at the bull from the safety of a tree until it decided it had seen enough and wandered off back into the scrub.

About three weeks into our time at Buchanan Downs I was headed down to the trapping yard for the umpteenth time when I saw an old cow that looked drunk. It was staggering along, slowly swaying on its feet. I thought it was because she was old but as I rode up to another small mob one of the bigger steers was wobbling the same way. It reminded me of a documentary I'd seen about herds of elephants and other animals in Africa that for a few weeks every year ate fermented fruit that had fallen out of trees, got drunk and staggered around like it was Saturday night.

After I finished penning the mob into the holding yard I went back to camp and told Chris about it. Chris said, 'This can't be good.' We told Rob about it when he turned up the next day. 'I'll get the vet. It must be bloody T.B. again,' he said angrily as he stormed back to his truck and drove away in a cloud of dust. In one of Chris' uncharacteristically serious moments he displayed his intellectual side by explaining to me that Bovine Tuberculosis was a scourge for cattlemen in the Territory. It showed up as lumps in the throat and caused difficulty breathing and a raspy cough (to me this sounded a lot like what old Ray was going through). Cattle would lose their appetite, become weak and often finally die. The disease could set back sales for months. It could take months to show and was easily spread between feral cattle and buffalo and domestic stock.

The government had started an eradication program that required all station managers to report any cases of T.B. in their herds, and an infected beast had to be put down and the rest of its mob quarantined. Stockies tested suspect mobs to help get rid of the disease completely. Cattle had to be injected just under the tail, held for three days and then checked for lumps as reactions. Any 'reactors' would be recorded, then shot and burned.

The next day the boss arrived with the vet who'd flown in from Katherine. Ray and a couple of other ringers turned up in two other station four-wheel-drives and the day got really busy. They headed off to find the sick cow from the day before, with the vet riding up front with Rob in the Tojo and Chris and I up on the back giving directions. We came first to the sick cow that was now lying down on her side and breathing heavily. The vet jumped out and went over to her with what looked like a plastic fishing tackle box. I couldn't see what was happening but I assume that the vet was drawing blood for testing later. The vet walked back to the driver's side window and discussed options with Rob. 'You know what to do,' he said clearly. 'Bugger,' said Rob as he unhooked his rifle from the racks on the back window and walked over to the old cow, loading a shell as he walked.

Afterwards he explained to the ringers that they should spread out around the Buchanan camp and find as many sick cattle as they could. They were to shoot anything 'wobbly' and drag it back to the spot where they were standing, and then burn the lot. He said, 'Do whatever you have to do to bring them down, then put them out as quick as you can.' Then he took the vet back to Murranji for his return to Katherine.

We spent the rest of the day chasing down sick cows and the odd steer. For a couple that were still mobile we drove alongside and roped them then shot them and dragged them away with a chain around a back leg. I spent the day with Mungo and Dave in Dave's truck. We found two small mobs with two visibly sick cows, and had to rope one of them to the Tojo, but the other was too far gone and just sat there as I walked up and put her out with one shot. By late afternoon we'd shot five and Dave dragged them all back to the pile.

While Dave was away I went for a short walk through a stand of scrub to have a look around for more. I came across another sick animal — a large steer. It was sitting on its front legs breathing heavily as I pulled another cartridge from my pocket and walked over. Then it stood up. It still had some life and energy in reserve. I stopped. The beast snorted, shook itself and gingerly started moving towards me as I stood there with an empty gun and a shell in my hand. I turned and ran and the steer gained a surprisingly quick amount of pace. I could hear the pounding of hooves close behind but then the beast stumbled, tripped over a rock and slid to a stop, fully spent. I was much more cautious on my second attempt as I walked carefully towards it, knelt on one knee, took aim and fired. Dave and Mungo heard the shot and drove over to find me with the last of the sick cattle. We used drums of diesel to burn the pile of carcasses, and we could see the black smoke rising up into the clear sky for a full day.

Rob and the other ringers stayed with us at the camp for two days. We trapped the rest of the paddock and then the others walked them back to the main yards for three days worth of testing when the vet came back from Katherine. We didn't have any more trouble with T.B. that year — none we knew of anyway. So long as there were wild mobs running around the outback there was a chance that the disease was just waiting to break out and give station managers more grief.

It was August by the time Chris and I cleaned up the camp at Buchanan Downs, packed all the gear into Mitch's truck and headed for the homestead once again. We'd trapped eight hundred head of healthy cattle and we'd shot and burned nine sick ones. I was glad to get back to the quarters, to a change in socks, a slight change in diet and a soft mattress. Saturday night beer tasted pretty good too.

'You can get clues to a cow's mood and condition by observing the tail. When the tail is hanging straight down, the cow is relaxed, grazing, or walking, but when the tail is tucked between the cow's legs, it means the animal is cold, sick, or frightened. When galloping, the tail is held straight out, and a kink can be observed when the animal is in a bucking, playful mood.'

Why and how to read a cow or bull,
Jack Albright 2000

CHAPTER 12
A Break In The Trail

I was headed for Elliott on another run for perishables. Amazingly I was still driving the same blue Tojo I'd used all season for my trips to town, but I still carried all the water and spares needed to make it to Elliott and back. The old truck was getting predictable. Depending on the outside temperature of the day I knew within about five minutes when I'd have to pull off the track, find a shady tree and turn the engine off to let it cool down before I could continue.

On this trip the Tojo decided to mix things up a bit and it overheated just near the turnoff at the Stuart Highway. I stopped under a tree, turned the engine off and sat there gazing down the long straight stretch of bitumen as I listened to the quiet hiss from the Tojo's radiator letting off steam. I watched tourists drive past in station wagons and motor homes, and ringers in utes and tray-backs. Most drivers slowed down and yelled at me through an open window, checking to see if I was okay.

I could see waves of heat rising from the hot ground and far away down the highway I could see something coming — walking up the side of the road. I got out and squinted south. It might have been a small mob that had got through the fence and out onto the road, but as I watched they came closer and got clearer in my vision. It was three men and four camels. They peeled off the highway and headed towards the treeline to come over and say hello.

The men in the camel team were from all over the Territory. Men dressed in canvas camouflage gear with wide-brimmed hats and easy smiles. The camels were packed lightly, no nonsense. Wet canvas water bags hung at every possible anchor point from what looked like purpose-built saddles sitting atop the camel's humps. The few brightly coloured little tassels and bells that jingled from the forehead leather of the halters stood out as extreme folly against the otherwise khaki outfit.

They enjoyed the shade of the tree and the break from the track as the camels awkwardly sat down and the men leant on the Tojo and introduced themselves. More of those tough handshakes. But I was getting better at it, I didn't even wince anymore. They were on the first leg of a 'short hop' from Renner Springs to the Buchanan Highway and on up to Daly Waters. The journey was a trial run in preparation for a much larger mission to travel by camel train from Darwin to Adelaide, as part of the Bicentennial Year Celebrations beginning early the next year.

One of the team was a young bloke who'd spent some time in Sydney. I asked him 'whereabouts?' and the recruit said he was born in Newcastle but moved to Waitara and went to school in Hornsby. 'Small world,' I said. I'd grown up in that area also. My birthplace was a central-west coal-mining town but my parents moved the family to Sydney when I was a toddler. I thought about that old saying then, 'you can take the boy out of the bush but you can't take the bush out of the boy...' and I thought about Sydney and mum working two jobs and long hours to keep the big house with the big mortgage. The early years with dad were not clear because he'd left home before I turned nine. The family sometimes referred to him kindly as a 'free spirit' but he was also a pharmacist, a minister of the church, a saxophone player and a rogue.

It was mum who survived the terrible teenage years, the fights, the problems and the fun times. Mum buckled down and worked hard to bring up two young boys and look after two elderly parents, while dad travelled the world. At the time it seemed like my old man was an exotic relative who did amazing things like hitchhiking across America, then spending years as a missionary in Southern Sudan. He'd fly into remote villages, hand out penicillin and Panadol, then bibles and songbooks.

Every so often he came back to Australia and he'd take my brother and I to Taronga Zoo or on a boat ride in Sydney Harbour and tell stories about other countries and other families. Not the best family model, but I liked the way things had turned out. I'd become independent and self-reliant. Here I was in the middle of the Northern Territory, driving down the Stuart Highway in a rusty station Tojo with the sun baking my forearm and a smile on my face. I was smiling a lot lately.

Mary welcomed me into the Elliott Store as if I was family. She even made a show of personal affection by thumping me on the arm with force and saying loudly, 'Well look here Ron, it's one of those fair dinkum ringers from Murranji. Not like those show ponies that came in yesterday.' She talked of a truckload of 'Darwin cowboys' that came into the store asking directions to Lake Woods. How they wore fancy shirts and big shiny belt buckles, they'd bought some worms and 'talked like wankers.'

Ron helped me load the Tojo with supplies and I caught up on what had been going on in Elliott the last few weeks, 'Much of the same same,' said Ron, but then he told me some interesting news: 'There's been a crazy tourist running around shooting people. Last seen in Katherine and they reckon he's heading south. They call him the Kimberley Killer.'

'Bloody hell,' I said in reply. 'Don't get shot,' I called back at Ron as I jumped into the truck.

'Mary's more dangerous than any bloody tourist,' Ron yelled back.

As I drove away I looked in the mirror and saw an angry Mary waving a fist and faintly heard another tirade of expletives at a smiling Ron.

I got back to the workmen's quarters just in time for dinner, and dinner was pretty special that night. I'd bought a large tub of triple-flavoured ice cream while I was at the store, certain it would go down a treat with the ringers. Ray cooked that night. I liked it when he cooked. Ray reckoned a ringer worked on his stomach, 'Like a good working horse,' he used to say. 'Feed 'em well, give 'em a treat now and then and they'll gallop all day for you.'

Ray tackled his cooking the same way he tackled everything else — with uncomplicated enthusiasm. He didn't have a lot in the kitchen cupboards but he had a nice little vegie garden going out behind the workmen's quarters and what he had he used to perfection. That night we gorged on braised beef, homegrown vegetables and garlic potatoes with ice cream for dessert.

There were some happy ringers lying around after dinner that evening, and there was one extra, 'Big Mick.' Big Mick was a rodeo rider from Mount Isa who had a big Stetson hat, a big brass belt buckle and a big blue Ford. He had big hands, big boots and a big voice as he told wild stories about riding wild bulls that only Big Mick could ride. Luckily he was a nice bloke because if he put his mind to it he could do you some big damage.

Big Mick was at Murranji looking for a couple of week's horse-work to save some money so he could enter in the saddle bronc and bull-riding events at the Daly Waters Rodeo. 'There's never been a horse or bull or woman born that I couldn't ride,' he used to say, with a big laugh. Big Mick was going to be working the new station horses with Mal while the rest of us broke up into gangs and went fixing fences around the long paddocks to the north.

The next day Chris and I were teamed up with Jimmy and given instructions to pack our swags and head out to Buchanan to meet a fencing gang. We had about fifteen kilometres of fence to build and two weeks to do it. We packed lightly, we didn't need much. Rob said the fencing gang had everything we needed, and we left soon after. I noticed that Jimmy had thrown a big role of baling twine into the tray. That seemed a little unusual, seeing as how we were going fencing, not hay baling. 'You'll find out,' was all Jimmy said.

We were halfway there when Jimmy yelled at Chris to stop driving and jumped out of the Tojo and took off running before the vehicle came to rest. He was moving fast, kicking up little puffs of dust from his heels as he ran. When he was fifty metres away he dove onto the ground and his hat flew off and rolled away. Chris and I were out of the truck by this time and wondering what Jimmy was up to when he stood up and proudly held aloft a squirming goanna, yelling at us that he was cooking tea that night. Jimmy tied the goanna's legs together and shoved it down between two of the swags on the back. 'You boys are in for a treat,' he said as he climbed back on board.

That wasn't the only unscheduled stop that we made on the way to Buchanan that day. Another couple of kilometres down the track and Chris stopped to take a piss. He walked about twenty metres away and stopped. It was pretty quiet out there. I was making another rollie as I listened to the flies buzzing against the windscreen and the far off sound of cockatoos chatting to each other in the trees. Chris was taking his sweet time. It seemed like minutes. I looked over and Chris was just standing there. 'Come on Chris,' I called. No answer.

Then Jimmy came to life. He grabbed the shovel as he jumped off the tray and ran straight at Chris. 'Bloody hell,' I said as I jumped out and started over in the same direction. Chris still hadn't moved. Jimmy raised the shovel as he ran. Then 'Wack!' Jimmy smashed the shovel at the ground as Chris jumped backwards. I arrived and looked down and saw two halves of a fat, evil-looking snake. 'It's a King Brown,' said Jimmy as he picked up the two bits. 'Second course,' he said smiling a big smile as we walked back to the Tojo to continue what had become an outback shopping trip.

'Why didn't you run?' I asked, and Chris explained that when you're that close to the most poisonous snake in the world the best thing you can do is act like a tree and they'll forget you're there. 'If you jump around they'll get you for sure,' he said. The King Brown (or 'Mulga snake' which is actually a member of the black snake family) is the meanest and most deadly reptile around. And they're fast. 'You don't want to get bitten out here,' said Jimmy, 'You're dead in twenty minutes. Ten if you get bit on the neck.' Chris casually remarked to me that I might as well roll a smoke and make peace with my maker because you 'don't have a whore's chance in heaven' if that happens to you way out there. 'That's what the baling twine is for' said Jimmy. 'We're gonna make hammocks to get us up off the ground and away from the King Browns.'

'Bloody good idea,' I said as I looked at the snake's eyes and big fangs and for the rest of the year, when I was walking around in the scrub I spent a lot less time looking around at the trees and the sky and the birds and much more looking at the ground.

We made it out to the campsite at Buchanan with no more excitement by about mid-afternoon, and set up camp near Buchanan Bore. Jimmy started weaving his hammock between two trees, using a couple of strong sticks at each end and the baling twine. He started with ten long lengths stretching between the trees and around the sticks, and then made a crosshatch pattern along the length of the hammock as a wide net to support his swag. Chris and I quickly picked up the pattern and within a couple of hours we had all three swags safely suspended in hammocks and covered with wide pieces of mozzie mesh to keep the bugs out.

The goanna tasted a bit greasy and the snake was overdone in the coals of the fire, but I enjoyed both very much. I once again wondered what else Murranji had in store as I lay gently swaying in my five star accommodation under my million-star night sky. In the distance I heard a dog howl over the sound of Chris snoring and the soft creaking of the baling twine around the tree. The last embers of the campfire were still glowing, and there was a slight breeze rustling the leaves in the tree as I drifted off to dream about snakes and goannas and cockatoos and campfires.

'Good morning sunshine!' said the booming voice. 'What's for bloody breakfast?' A rough leathery face was beaming at me about twelve inches from my nose. The sun was up. I must have slept in. 'Come on sunshine, the day's nearly over,' said the stranger as he walked over to stoke the fire and put the billy back on the coals. I looked around and could see Chris and Jimmy over the other side of the camp talking to another stranger leaning on the tray of an old red Hino truck. The man at the fire introduced himself as 'Paddy' and asked me if I was ready to do some serious fencing work. 'That is of course if you ever get yourself out of the cot,' he laughed. For the next three weeks the old fencing contractor always referred to me as 'Sleepy.'

'Like one of those seven dwarfs from the story 'bout the pretty girl and the poison apple,' he said.

CHAPTER 13
The Long Fence

The dingoes approached from the east. There were about six of them, but they were not all dingoes. I couldn't tell what breed some of them were but two were bigger, darker than the rest, German Shepherds or some other big breed. And one of them was small, like a terrier.

They came out of the trees about four hundred metres from where I was working. I'd been slowly walking along the fence line tying plastic 'droppers' onto the three strands of barb wire every five metres or so. Jimmy and Chris were about three hundred metres up the fence line in the other direction, ramming in another steel post. The dogs kept coming. They were moving with purpose, as though they had somewhere to go, something to do. Paddy and his offsider, Spud, were out of sight somewhere up the fence line on the other side of the dogs.

I suddenly felt very alone, naked. One of the bigger dogs stopped and looked straight at me. The others stopped for a couple of seconds, then kept coming, trotting along with their tails swaying left and right. I held a handful of plastic droppers that are great for keeping three barb wires evenly spaced apart but pretty hopeless at fending off anything larger than a bunny rabbit.

I also possessed a pocketknife in a pouch on my belt that was great at slicing open a ball sack but not much good at anything serious. I longed for a rifle, any rifle.

The dogs kept coming. They looked even more determined than before, and they looked hungry. I felt like a deer caught in headlights. I really wasn't sure what to do. Should I run? Where to? Should I stand there and wave my hands around like a crazy man and jump up and down? I thought briefly that it'd probably be best to start singing. That would scare them off for sure. Then I heard the crack of a rifle and saw the dog in front fall. The others scattered and ran.

Paddy was at the edge of the trees, rifle in his hands and down on one knee. He had another couple of shots at the galloping dogs but missed each time. He got up and started walking over towards the fallen animal and I started in that direction as well. We met at the dog — a big mangy-looking crossbred. It was not breathing and a small pool of blood was gathering in the dust just under its shoulder.

'That was a bloody good shot hey' said Paddy without question. 'It must have been two fifty. And on the trot away from me as well,' he said. I asked, 'What would they have done?' I was wondering if this was another one of my lucky days. Paddy explained how bastard tourists let their pet dogs go by the side of the road because they didn't want to keep looking after them as they travelled around. The strays would then cross-breed with other wild mongrels and part-dingoes, and they turned nasty. They could kill calves and Paddy had even seen one wild pack bring down a small steer. 'Maybe they would have helped themselves to a bit of Sleepy,' he said with a laugh as he walked away, leaving the dead mongrel dog for the crows. 'Keep going kid, we've got another hundred posts to put in today. Another couple of kilometres of barb.' And that's what we did that day. And the next day, and the next.

Fifteen kilometres in three weeks. We ran three strands at a time. The wire was fed from three posts on the back of the Hino truck as Spud drove it along the fence line. A steel post was rammed into the ground every twenty-five metres and then three plastic droppers were tied on in between. Not much of a fence really, you could push through it pretty easily. Spud used to say they were more like guidelines than fence lines.

Spud had been Paddy's offsider for as long as he could remember. He didn't know how old he was and he couldn't remember many happy times from his childhood. Before he ran into Paddy he'd been bounced from one family to another. I assumed he'd been a child of the foster-care system. He'd met Paddy in a fencing camp near Katherine when he ran away from his latest mum and dad. Paddy gave him a swag, a pair of fencing gloves and three square meals a day. Well, a decent dinner at night time, the chance of a quick feed at lunchtime and the occasional breakfast. Most mornings he had what they call a 'stockman's breakfast' — a piss and a look about. But Spud was happy with his lot. He couldn't remember the last time he was in Katherine and didn't care. He loved travelling the country, laying down fence lines and sleeping rough.

'They can keep their houses, their television sets and their air-conditioning,' he said one day as he was teaching me how to do a nifty 'figure-of-eight' knot to join two long lengths of wire together. 'But what about girls?' I asked. 'More trouble than a mickey bull,' Spud replied and Chris said, 'Too right, who needs females anyway?' while thinking how absolutely delicious a girlfriend would be.

That night it was my turn to cook. I knocked off early from the fencing job and headed back to camp to start tea. I started the fire, put on a big pot of water to boil and started chopping vegetables and meat. I had damper mixed up pretty quickly and set the camp oven in the hole next to the fire, ready for the doughy mix. A couple of hot coals around the edge of the old camp oven, dust the inside with flour and bung the damper mix in. I put the lid on, covered the top with a shovel-full of hot coals and then buried the lot with dirt. One and a half hours later I dug it all up and served the men steaming slices of fresh bushie bread with a bowl full of cowboy casserole and a cup of billy tea.

'Not bad,' said Paddy as he dipped his damper into the last of his stew, 'Not bad at all.' I didn't look over at Paddy as he spoke. I didn't much enjoy looking over at Paddy when he was sitting on the other side of the fire on one of the rough old canvas camp chairs. Paddy didn't believe in wearing any underwear but he did believe in wearing baggy, loose-fitting shorts. It just didn't seem right to me that a man should let it all hang out that way. I reckoned a man should keep his meat and two veg' locked away from sight until needed.

But to Paddy it all seemed natural. Like his attitude. He was a real natural bloke. If he were any more relaxed about life he'd be asleep. He told stories about growing up in the Gulf country around Borroloola and Macarthur River. At age six he was navigating an old dingy out in the mangroves catching barramundi bigger than he was tall. He built himself a humpy when he was thirteen, shot his first buffalo at fifteen and driving road trains all over the Northern Territory at seventeen.

He loved Borroloola. He called it his 'second heaven.' In fact, the town had a reputation of being home to criminals and alcoholics — one of the last real frontier towns. In the special way that myth becomes legend in the Territory the town became a rite of passage for young men up there. He said that you weren't a true Territorian until you had been barra' fishing and bar room brawling in Borroloola.

Paddy said that he'd lived with the blackfellas around Borroloola for a while. There were four different tribes living in and around the town — the Mara and Yanyuwa people, who were referred to as 'saltwater people' and the Kurdunji and Karawa, 'people of the land.' Borroloola sat on both sides of the Macarthur River and for most of the inhabitants the local sport, food, playtime and income was fishing. Paddy said his happiest memories were drifting down the river dragging a silver lure behind a wooden canoe and catching barra. Or catching big, shiny mud crabs for dinner. I thought mud crabs would have been a welcome change in diet right about then, but I was a long way from the muddy riverbanks of Borroloola. Camp stew, damper and billy tea had to do for now.

We got into another nice routine. We woke at sunrise, went for a wash in the dam, boiled the billy for coffee and ate damper covered thick in vegemite. We'd head off down the fence line to where we'd finished the day before and resume our jobs, as if we'd been doing it for years. Spud set up another three rolls of barbwire to be fed off down the track that had been bulldozed years earlier in a gun barrel line heading northwest. The rest of us pounded steel posts into the ground, tied the barb on with short lengths of plain wire, and then the last bloke in the line tied on the plastic droppers at even intervals.

Paddy came along in the station truck feeding posts and droppers to the rest of us as we worked. One day it was Jimmy's turn to follow along behind and tie the droppers on. As the day wore on the heat began to build. It must have been nearly forty degrees by mid-morning. We moved far ahead of Jimmy down the fence line. I looked back in Jimmy's direction and could vaguely see his hat moving through the heat haze. We stopped and lit a fire and boiled the billy for tea at lunchtime and an hour later we stopped again.

We had to do some extra work over a steep little gully and I looked back and saw Jimmy faintly through the dust, his hat still jiggling on his head. Paddy looked that way as well and remarked that the little bloke was a real hard worker indeed. 'He hasn't stopped to rest all day long,' he said as he threw another couple of steel posts at my feet. By mid-afternoon we'd covered about three kilometres and Paddy decided we'd done enough for the day. We packed up and headed back up the fence line to pick up Jimmy and go for a swim in the dam to cool down. We got within about a kilometre of Jimmy and could see his hat still bobbing away on his pointy head. Chris remarked again what a bloody hard worker he was to still be going at it this late in the day, but as we got nearer we realised the truth. We drove up to Jimmy's hat, neatly placed on top of a steel post, and we looked over to a nearby shady tree and saw the underside of Jimmy's R.M. Williams boots sticking out of the grass. As we walked over noisily Jimmy raised his sleepy head and asked, 'lunchtime yet?'

'Smart bugger,' said Spud. 'It's nearly bloody dinner time and you haven't tied a dropper on all day.'

'Sorry boss,' Jimmy replied, 'I just lay down for minute and must have dozed off. I was having a really nice dream about a girl I met at a rodeo. It took me ages to win her over with my boyish charms. You wouldn't want to me to disturb me doing that now would you?' he said as we all clambered back onto the truck for the ride back to camp.

It was Spud's turn to cook that night. He set himself to the task with gusto, madly mixing damper and chopping a side of corned beef like a demon. We swam in the dam, organised more firewood and spent time fixing tools and getting ready for the next day's fencing. During quiet times round an outback campfire ringers like to do three things; sharpen their knives, twist up spare lashes for their stockwhips and play the game of 'Stick.'

Stick involves twenty-one different ways of spinning your pocketknife so it sticks nicely upright in the dirt at your feet. Sometimes you hold the very tip out in front and let it spin backwards and other times you rest the point on your upturned elbow and flick it forwards. The hardest trick of all is number twenty-one where you throw it over your shoulder and see if you can stick it into the ground close to the heel of your boots without slicing flesh off your calf muscle at the same time. Ringers are good at sharpening their pocketknives because they spend a lot of time putting an edge back on their blades after every game of Stick.

Later that evening Jimmy showed me some of the secrets of tracking animals in the dirt. He smoothed out a big area with the side of his hand and used his fingers and palms to expertly recreate the tracks of local wildlife. He did dingo tracks, emu, goanna and plains turkey tracks. Then he used a straight hand and pushed the dust left and right to represent a snake on the move.

Jimmy had grown up around Murranji. He was born in Halls Creek to the northwest and his family had moved around the country, living for periods of time at Murranji, in Katherine and in Tennant Creek. When he was old enough he bought an old car and drove back to Murranji.

Ever since he could remember Jimmy had been around horses. His father was a well-known ringer and horse-breaker who worked on many stations in the Kimberley and Territory. He had a reputation as a 'gun' rider who could stick like glue. He possessed those natural skills for roping and mustering that were most valuable to station managers up there. They say indigenous stockmen were the backbone of the early cattle industry in the Top End as it grew from harsh and humble beginnings to the massive business it has become.

Blackfella-stockmen once worked for months at a time in outback droving teams or on outback cattle stations, living simply and working hard. Then they'd go to town and spend long days with family and friends, fishing and swimming and hunting. Jimmy loved those old days. He remembered long hot days tailing mobs of cattle with his father. Learning how to think like a cow, how to crack his stockwhip properly and how to rope a young bull at flat gallop. Everyone had a job to do and no time to get into trouble.

After a while Jimmy made his own mark, and his reputation was well established. He was respected by the boss and looked up to by all the other would-be ringers. But Jimmy's father hadn't seen it for a long time. He was stuck in town and drunk most of the time. He'd long ago sold his saddle to buy grog and spent most days sitting around the campfire at the back of the pub at Elliott, and most nights inside getting wasted. Jimmy explained to me there wasn't much he could do about it.

Every three months or so Jimmy was paid out by Rob and went to town to be with his father. He gave him money, helped him buy food and cooked meals for him. He took him fishing again. They spent a few weeks together and then Jimmy came back to work at Murranji. 'There's not much else to do in town,' he said, 'And grog is cheap.'

The next day we finished the fencing job and helped Paddy and Spud pack the camp gear, stack all the remaining posts and wire, and then said goodbye. Paddy's last bit of advice was as surprising as it was disturbing, 'Remember to piss on your hands. It'll toughen them up for sure.' I never found out if that little gem was just another ringer's joke or not.

I looked back at the campsite as we drove away. There was no familiar trail of smoke rising up out of the now-cold campfire. The black baling twine hammocks hung empty in the trees, like fishnet stockings cast aside by a giant pole-dancing stripper. Paddy's truck was slowly moving away in the opposite direction and I could see Spud's sunburnt elbow hanging out the window as he rolled another cigarette.

We drove along the new fence for a couple of kilometres to the south, then went through the brand new Queensland gate we'd built just a few days earlier. The three of us were quiet as we drove. Even though we were tired and sore after weeks of work we were going to miss the fencing camp. Well, I was going to look back and think fondly of my time at Buchanan, but maybe the novelty had worn off for the other two.

CHAPTER 14
Families Lost and Found

I was happy to be driving towards Elliott again. I had four hundred dollars and I was thinking how I would spend it. Last time I was in Mary's shop I'd seen a really nice new roo-hide stockwhip and a pair of tan Red Wing boots. Mitch had asked me to pick up a couple more tins of Log Cabin tobacco, his favourite, and Mal was hoping I could smuggle a bottle of bourbon back to camp, 'for medicinal purposes.' I was more than happy to oblige on both counts. My passenger that day did not seem as jovial. All the way to town Jimmy sat and stared through the windscreen as we bumped along.

I pulled up at the camp behind the pub and shut off the engine. When I stepped out of the driver's door, five mangy mongrel dogs came barking and snapping at my boots and Jimmy ran around from his side of the Tojo to help me kick them in the guts. I looked around and took it all in. There was garbage strewn everywhere. Hundreds, maybe thousands of beer cans and old wine casks scattered right across the camp. There was one main fire pit in the middle and there were a number of smaller fires smoking around the perimeter. Here and there across the camp was an old mattress or piece of canvas and a couple of old camp chairs. The only structures in sight were things that resembled what used to be steel-framed fibro homes. Long ago they had windows and walls and doors, but were now skeleton structures with flat tin roofs awkwardly balanced on top.

There were about thirty people of different ages moving or sitting around the campsite. Some kids were playing in the dirt in front of the Tojo with what looked like the tail of a kangaroo and there was a small group of old ladies sitting cross-legged chattering away at each other as they absently shooed flies away. Jimmy's mum materialized from one of the humpies and came quickly over to give her son a hug. He brushed her aside as she staggered to him and went forward to find his father. 'My Jimmy's home,' I heard her say as she followed her son back into the humpy.

I looked over towards the two old blokes sitting on a big log at the other side of the campfire and headed over to sit down. One of the men looked up and smiled a toothless grin as I sat down and with a thick accent said, 'You Murranji ringer hey? You friend of Jimmy's?' he asked. 'Yes I am,' I answered genuinely. 'Then you friend of mine,' said the old man as he went back to making a thin rollie and poking a stick into the fire to light up his cigarette. 'You know what young fella?' he said when he'd got his rollie going properly. 'I bin a ringer on Murranji long, long time before now. Long before I could walk I bin tailing Murranji steers,' he said. 'I've taught lots of young whitefellas like you to ride like a ringer.'

The other old bloke who was slumped beside him came to life then, and muttered something about cattle and the bullwaddy and desert. He stood up with an effort that made him breathe a bit harder and he walked away, scratching at something that was biting him below his belt. My new friend and I sat there for a while making and smoking rollies, poking the fire and listening to the women chatter and the kids yell and play. One of the little kids ran up to me and leant his naked black torso on my knee. He pointed with a dirty finger at the Tojo and said, 'That your truck?'

'Sure is,' I answered. 'You want to go for a drive?' Half an hour later I had Jimmy and Jimmy's dad in the front seat with three kids, three women and the two old blackfellas up on the back as we all headed for Lake Woods to catch dinner. Along the way we picked up another family walking the track and stopped to grab some bait. The blokes knew exactly where to dig to get handfuls of grubs and wriggly insects and the women set handlines with rusty hooks up and down the bank. I spent the rest of the afternoon on an old punt, fishing for yellow belly with Jimmy's family and friends in the dark cool water at Lake Woods.

After we got back to the camp at Elliott we cooked the fish for tea and had a cup of sweet billy tea. Then I excused myself, thanked them all and went to the pub. That night I got really drunk. I won a hundred dollars on the pool table from two noisy jackaroos and lost about the same amount over the bar for beer and bourbon. I chatted for a while to a road train driver on his way to Darwin with a load of washing machines and air-conditioners. The bloke had a beer-gut the size of a beanbag and he held it in place with an old Balmain Tigers footy jumper. His favourite team. We talked about women and driving trucks and drinking and driving trucks. The driver said he was leaving Darwin in three days time with a return load for Adelaide, then the following day he was going to be turning around and driving straight back with another load of consumables for eager Darwin shoppers.

The television was on over the bar. The ABC was running an item about the Kimberley Killer running around the outback shooting people here and there, and then moving on. The Northern Territory Police had few clues but lots of rumors and false sightings. They had one survivor who'd provided them with a vague description of the killer's car and the fact that he had a German accent. But the Top End was a huge place and it was easy to get lost up there. This reality was reinforced in the next feature item that came on the little television above the publican's head.

Wayward travelers had been found dead, perished in the desert. 'That could be me lying there,' I thought as I sat in the air-conditioned bar with ice in my bourbon and a new pair of Red Wing boots on my feet. I wondered where all my luck was coming from, and how long it was going to last. I slept in the back of the Tojo that night, buried deep in my swag against the chill, and the next morning I headed back to Murranji.

I drove into the compound as a little white Cessna was bumping along the airstrip towards the workshop. Rob met me as I pulled up and told me to put the groceries away, then come over and meet his uncle 'Roy,' the man who had just flown over for a visit. Roy was one of two brothers who owned another station near the little town of Daly Waters, up the track towards Katherine. Daly Waters was famous for two things, an explorer's tree and a rodeo. The tree was supposedly where in 1862 the legendary explorer John McDouall

Stuart carved his initial 'S.' If you drink lots of beer, cock your head to one side and look long and hard you can see the letter S unclearly.

Like the Birdsville races, the Henley-on-Todd dry-river yacht race, and the Borroloola Barra Classic, the Daly Waters Rodeo is legendary across Australia. Even if you've never travelled through the area you've probably heard about the event. Cowboys come a thousand miles or more to ride bulls and saddle broncs at Daly Waters. Others try to impress the judges, and the ladies, at camp drafting, steer roping and bareback riding.

Roy and his brother grew up on large cattle stations in Queensland and the Northern Territory and were well known in the district. Somehow the two men had overcome those naturally competitive issues that usually cause problems between siblings, and against all the challenges Mother Nature could throw at them they worked out how to combine their talents to grow some of the best beef cattle in the Territory. They'd just been through one of the driest decades on record (1970s) and experienced huge hikes in interest rates, which caused beef markets to collapse. But they moved cattle around the Territory onto good grass, and stayed afloat. Altogether the family managed a staggering amount of stock over many thousands of square kilometres of outback country, and with the use of road trains they could move thousands of cattle across the region within days. Rob introduced me to his uncle as 'one of my best men' and I grew four inches that day. We chatted about cattle prices and the cost of diesel and the weather and the latest news about the Kimberley Killer. As he and Rob walked off towards the big house Roy said to me, 'See you at the rodeo next month.'

'No worries,' I replied, 'I'm looking forward to it.'

Rob rounded up all the ringers after the plane flew out and told us that the next day we were all going to drive out to Ucharonidge Station to fill a couple of road trains with hay. Rob explained that the grass was extra long out there that season, much more than they needed for their own stock. Five tractors had been going around in circles for three weeks mowing, raking and baling. It was all hands on deck for the loading and unloading. The Murranji crew was going to leave before sun-up the next day to bring back thousands of the little square bundles of feed.

We were woken at four o'clock and most of the men spread swags in the back of the trucks and settled down for a cold bumpy ride. I rode up front in Mitch's four-wheel-drive. As we drove we listened to old country songs like

'Leave him out there in the longyard,' and 'Pub with no beer,' on his cassette player. It was going to be a long day. A hot day. It was the day I turned twenty-three.

Our Andy's gone to battle now 'gainst drought, the red marauder. Our Andy's gone with cattle now across the Queensland border. He's left us in dejection now. Our hearts with him are roving. It's dull on this selection now since Andy went a-droving'

Andy's Gone With Cattle,
Henry Lawson 1888

CHAPTER 15
All Baled Up

We drove into the rising sun, turned south along the Stuart Highway, then east again across the Barkly Stockroute. The sky turned purple, then orange, then yellow. Birds flew across the sky, silhouetted black in the morning light. I felt the morning chill on my elbow as we headed east.

There were twelve men in total. Rob led the convoy with Ray riding shotgun in the passenger seat and Walter and another ringer asleep on the tray in the back. Mitch and I followed with another two sleeping bodies and Mal drove the horse truck with the remaining three ringers bouncing around in various stages of sleep. Mungo was sitting up next to Mal in the cab telling him stories about his time working on an outback drilling rig. The morning reminded him of times when the gang was heading for a new drilling site in the early hours, with the trucks fully loaded with men and long lengths of bore-casing and tools. They travelled all over the South Australian gas fields, working here and there and then packing up and moving on to the next job.

Mungo told Mal about the hot days running bore-casing down a hole and the cold nights exhausted, sleeping like a baby. 'At twenty stone that's one bloody big baby,' Mal said as he drove. I wasn't sleepy. I was wide-awake and staring out the windscreen at the wide open road ahead. I thought about the Triffids' song that was played to death on the radio the year before, 'The sky was big and empty, my chest filled to explode, I yelled my insides out at the sun, at the wide open road.'

We'd been driving east for two hours and the country had changed from hard scrub to endless miles of open Mitchell-grass plains. We were still many kilometres from Ucharonidge when the lead truck blew a front tyre and veered off the track. Rob fought the wheel as the truck slid sideways at an angle across the dirt road. I could see the men on the back gripping the side rails as they bounced around.

The truck came to rest facing backwards in the table drain on the side of the track. Rob got out and surveyed the men in the back. Walter sat up and said, 'That was close boss. Good thing Ray wasn't driving.' Ray reached into the tray to clip him over the ear and Walter made out like he was scared shitless. The whole convoy came to a halt, and we stood around making rollies and conversation as we provided much needed advice about changing tyres to the two poor blokes on their knees at the driver's side front wheel.

Two hours later we topped a rise and came upon two empty road trains, a couple of tractors and a landscape full of little rectangular brown bales of hay stretching in long wavy lines far off into the distance. We were in the northwest corner of the property and we had a big job to do. 'I want to be stacking in fifteen minutes!' Rob shouted as we pulled up next to the first truck. That was all it took to get started. Everyone automatically separated into two teams and we organised ourselves around the two road trains. Mal and Walter were barking orders as the road trains fired up their engines and slowly moved away in opposite directions next to the first row.

Beside each trailer ringers were walking along, throwing bales up to another ringer stationed in the trailer door who in turn passed them to another inside who stacked them in neat, tight rows. I enjoyed the first hour stacking hay bales on Ucharonidge Station. I told Ray as I passed him on one of the turns that it was 'a good day in the sunshine. Healthy exercise and clean air.'

Ray said, 'You're not going to feel that way three hours from now.' How right he was. By mid-afternoon I was about to pass out. The heat, the fine hay dust that got into your sweat, your eyes and your nose, and the crowded, low-roof compartments of the road trains became a living hell. And poor Big Mick was really feeling it. He must have lost three kilos in sweat that afternoon. By the third time I vomited I'd forgotten where I was. The hay bales just kept coming and coming. My hands ached and bleeding again. My back was screaming in protest. On another endless pass around Mal grabbed me, handed me a wet canvas water bag and ordered me to go lie down in the shade. I enjoyed the ten-minute break before dragging myself to my feet and joining the crew once more.

Halfway through the job a third road train arrived but I didn't notice. Blindly I walked along picking up bales and automatically throwing them up over my head to the waiting hands of the ringers at the doors of the nearest trailer. By late afternoon we'd filled all three trucks — nine double-deck trailers to the brim. We rode in the trucks up to the homestead, to showers, dinner and a cot for the night.

After breakfast next morning we were told we could relax around the homestead at Ucharonidge until lunchtime when we'd be heading back to Murranji. The Ucharonidge homestead and workshop were similar to Murranji except larger. The workmen's quarters were built to accommodate two-dozen jackaroos and ringers at any one time and the boss's house was a neat brick building with green lawns and a colourful garden.

I wandered around the compound chatting with the station ringers. Some of the Ucharonidge staff were jillaroos — female jackaroos. They said they mustered and fenced and did yard work just as good as the boys. One of the young jackaroos got a stockwhip lash to his legs when he said under his breath, 'bullshit,' just before he started running. The girls seemed to fit in at Ucharonidge. I couldn't see any evidence of the same female troubles we'd had at Murranji. Some of the ringers even admitted that the girls were 'half handy around cattle' and 'pretty good with the ponies.' Maybe it was because they didn't show off their bumps and grooves like Martin's girlfriend did. Instead they hid them under loose shirts and riding jeans.

I went to the workshop to chat with Mitch and the local mechanic who were leaning into an old station four-wheel-drive, discussing the merits of Toyota versus Nissan, and the latest hardware coming out of Japan. The mechanic introduced himself as 'Norm' and launched into a long and detailed explanation about the challenges of being an outback mechanic. With approving grunts and 'too rights' from Mitch, Norm said, 'Take this old Hino horse truck for instance. You don't just go down to the corner store and pick up the parts you need. You have to be resourceful.'

'Bloody-well right,' said Mitch.

After holding out a blackened and greasy hand for another tough outback handshake, Norm told me his only option to get the truck going again was to make a new push-rod for the engine out of an old trolley shaft. He had to heat it and cool it to temper it properly, then cut it and flatten out the end to fit into the lifters just right. He talked about the many hours lying under a broken road train gearbox in the hot sand and I asked him if they were hard to drive. Norm said simply, 'Come and I'll show you.'

A road train at Murranji Station, Northern Territory. Fully loaded with more than 120 weaners for market, these 'triples' can be more than 70m long and weigh 100 tonnes.

Half an hour later I was sitting in the driver's seat of a huge Mack Superliner prime mover shifting from seventh to eighth gear and once again feeling like the King of the World. For all its size, weight and horsepower I found the big truck easy to operate. The driver's seat was about ten feet off the ground and the exhaust stacks were blowing thick clouds of diesel smoke that could be seen trailing behind in the mirrors. The big steering wheel was covered with fluffy lambswool and the seat was like a Smokey Dawson Recliner on springs. I could see why men got hooked on trucks. The noise, the altitude. Mitch sat up in the cabin with us, helping explain all about special truck diffs and heavy duty clutches and gearboxes, all of which had been split open at some point and pulled apart on Norm's greasy workbench.

Norm knew every nut and bolt on the truck and he could have told Mitch and I all about every one if our time at Ucharonidge was not up. I thanked Norm as I climbed down out of the cabin and said I hoped I saw him at Murranji one day. As he walked away, Norm said, 'This place would fall apart in one hour without me.'

We drove out of Ucharonidge at around midday, turned south and headed home. Most of us held a sense of dread as we thought of the next part of the job coming up, unloading. We'd lived through the hell of loading the thousands of little square bales that after a while felt like they weighed two hundred kilos, and soon they all had to be handled again.

At least the following day was cooler and the unloading easier as we didn't have to walk the long paddocks, but simply form human chains from the trailers and pass hay bales to each other without having to bend down or walk to far. The worst part was when you got your turn at being one of the blokes moving bales around inside the low-roofed trailer compartments. Rob was so pleased at the job well done that he gave us all the next two days off. Most decided to spend their time and most of their money at the Elliott Hotel. Rob rang ahead to warn the publican that a bunch of rowdy ringers was headed his way. He gave the local cops a quick call as well, just to cover all bases.

'We're gonna rape the cows and stampede the women!' Chris yelled from the window of Mitch's truck as he sped past me and out of the compound on his way to town. I followed later with Big Mick in his Ford and when we came to the Stuart Highway Mick asked which way I wanted to go, 'North or south?' Over the last six months I must have made more than twenty trips to town. Every time I got to the end of the Murranji track at the Stuart I turned south and headed towards Elliott. This time I said, 'Left this time Mick.'

Twenty minutes later and we were surrounded by cops with weapons drawn and angry faces yelling at us. We'd been heading north for only ten minutes when a police jeep went past us going south with its lights and sirens blaring. We didn't think much about it at the time. We were chatting about bloody hay bales and the road trains and how we were going to spend our money at the Dunmarra Roadhouse. Mick didn't even notice the Police jeep in his mirrors do a fast U-turn. It dropped back to follow Mick's Ford at a distance.

Five minutes later and Mick noticed something strange on the highway up ahead. There was a white Police jeep parked sideways across the road with its blue lights flashing on the roof and a line of cars and caravans banked up behind it to the north. A roadblock. Mick then noticed the Police vehicle in his mirror when it turned on its own flashing blue lights. 'They must have radioed ahead,' he said to me as I leaned forward in my seat squinting, trying to make out what was going on up ahead. Mick stopped about fifty metres from the Police jeep and shut the engine off.

The jeep behind screeched to a stop facing sideways on the highway. I heard two car doors slam and I looked out through the back window to see two cops with weapons drawn advancing slowly towards us. The cops who were standing next to the jeep in front of Mick's truck started edging towards us as well. 'What the bloody hell did you do?' I quietly asked Mick who was sitting nervously in the driver's seat rolling his palms over the top of the steering wheel. 'It was a long time ago and a long way from here,' he replied. 'Shit,' I said as I contemplated my short but eventful life, and my imminent death.

'Get Out Slowly!' boomed a big voice from behind Mick's truck, 'and lie down on the road!' For a horrible second I thought that Big Mick was going to restart his truck and try to drive through the guns. Then I said, 'Come on Mick, get out of the bloody truck.'

'Righto' then,' was Big Mick's reply as we slowly opened our doors, held our hands above our heads and then lay down on the hot bitumen, face-first. The cops came up slowly, split into two pairs. Two of them held a gun at us on the ground while the other two approached, knelt down and shoved a knee into us. 'Hang on,' said one of the cops standing back, 'Is that you Andy?' I tried to speak, and swallowed loudly. I was sweating profusely. The road was really hot and the gravel hard on my bony hips, especially with a heavy Northern Territory copper sitting on me. 'Yep,' I squeaked, 'Yep, It's me.'

'Let 'em up,' said the cop. 'These fellas are Murranji ringers.' The cop who spoke was one I had seen in Elliott. We stood up and automatically dusted ourselves off while the cops explained the reason for our mistaken identity. They'd been given reports that morning that the Kimberley Killer had been spotted around Tenant Creek getting into a blue Ford. It was going to be a long busy day for the cops that day. I wondered how many blue Fords were travelling up and down the Stuart Highway that time of year, and estimated double digits.

The cops apologised as they walked back to their vehicles, jumped in and drove away in different directions. Big Mick and I were left standing in the middle of the road as the banked-up traffic started to move. 'Let's go get drunk,' Big Mick said as we climbed back into the truck. 'Good idea,' I said as we drove away, 'And then you can tell me why you were so nervous back there.'

If I hadn't drunk so much bourbon that evening I may have remembered exactly what it was that Big Mick had done in the past to make him so jumpy. Why it was that he broke out in a cold sweat. As it turned out, I couldn't even recollect how it was that we got back to Murranji the next day, alive and intact.

CHAPTER 16
Buckin' Out

The first three weeks of September were relatively quiet around Murranji homestead. Mal was down in the yards most days working two of the green station horses, walking them around with the long reins or riding them up and down the fencelines, working on their mouths and their minds. He took his time, he didn't rush. He explained to me one day as I was leaning on the yard rails, watching and still learning, 'Young horses need lots of hours of tedious quiet repetition to get them settled, get them used to you.'

Mitch spent most of his time in the workshop pulling an engine apart and rebuilding it with new pistons and rings. The engine was coming apart pretty easily so there wasn't much swearing or throwing tools. I spent some time there as well, helping and learning. I worked the hydraulic lifter as Mitch guided the motor down onto its mounts, and then I leant into the engine bay and helped hook up all the necessary hoses, pipes, wires and cables. We were covered in black grease and oil when Mitch turned the key to start it. We nodded in mutual satisfaction as we listened to the smooth ticking sound as it idled.

Big Mick, Chris, and some of the others mustered one of the paddocks near Mud Bore. Rob had put some of his better heifers out there and a cattle buyer was coming the next week to check them out for a sale to a property in the Kimberley region, far to the northwest of Murranji. Mungo and Walter and a couple of the other blackfellas were tailing a mob of cattle south of the homestead. Ray was repairing a couple of old Barcoo Poley saddles, fixing the seat leathers and sewing some blown stitching. In between long days trapping and tailing cattle around Number 4 Bore with some of the others, Dave and I were welding gates and rebuilding the second loading ramp at the main cattle yards. One of the younger road train drivers had reversed into it and pushed it over onto an awkward angle.

Rob spent his days driving around the station checking on the men and lending a hand or advice where necessary. Some nights he even came down to the workmen's quarters to have dinner with the men, and they'd play cards and listen to the little radio in the kitchen. During one especially good hand Chris wanted to bet his whole season's wages against Rob's best American saddle, but Rob said, 'How are you gonna buy girls if you lose?'

'Haven't you heard, I never lose,' he replied, and the others fell about laughing when the cards were laid out on the table. Chris nearly cried that evening and for the rest of the season he wondered if Rob was going to collect on his winnings, and the others had enormous fun at his expense.

Murranji only had one visitor in that time. One of Mal's cousins was on his way to Adelaide from Darwin for a wedding and he stopped in at Murranji to break the trip. It was lucky for him that he stopped over because he got tonnes of advice from all the ringers about what he should organise for his mate's buck's night. We sat around recounting stories of drunken parties where an unwitting groom had been completely humiliated in a hundred different ways. Mal had roped one poor guy naked to a tree, and Chris had helped his brother dance naked on stage at a strip club in Brisbane. For some reason there were a lot of stories involving drunk naked men. Dave had left his best friend chained to a telephone pole with a bowling ball padlocked to his ankle and Mungo had buried a groom up to his neck in beach sand. The poor bloke was then fed vodka through a hose and had his eyebrows shaved off. I didn't have any stories or advice about buck's nights to add to the others, but I was sure not looking forward to getting married.

I went to town twice in that three weeks and both trips were uneventful. I picked up extra tins of tobacco for the ringers, a new hat for Mungo (custom-made to fit his enormous head) and a new stockwhip for Dave. I dropped into the pub on the second trip and everyone was talking about the Daly Waters Rodeo. There were a couple of ringers from nearby Newcastle Waters Station who told me all about their big plans to enter the saddle bronc and bareback events to get warmed up for the big one, the bull-riding. They'd been practicing on steers at the Newcastle Waters yards and the boss let them ride some of the station buck-jumpers.

When I got back to Murranji I told Rob about the preparations going on at Newcastle Waters, and Rob decided 1987 was the year a Murranji ringer was going to win the bull-riding event. Everyone believed that it was going to be Big Mick, but everyone would have a go. We were all going to ride a steer or enter the calf-roping events so we spent the week leading up to the rodeo getting ready. Mal and Chris organised a practice area in the main yards for the team-roping event. Mitch helped them set up a small chute so we could release calves on the run for Mal and Chris to chase down and rope.

The two riders got ready on each side and then Mitch and I would push a young bull-calf out the chute to go galloping across the big yard. The horses leapt instantly into a full gallop with their riders swinging ropes above their heads. Mal expertly threw his lariat and roped one of the calf's back legs as Chris threw his to catch a front leg. The horses skidded to a stop and backed up to keep the tension on the ropes as if they'd been trained for years to do it that way. At the same time the men jumped off and threw the immobilised calf to the ground. They missed about half the time, but when they got it right it was a beautiful thing to watch.

Rob was positively happy. He was really enjoying himself. It had been a long time since he'd been able to forget about cattle prices, bovine diseases and the endless bills that came into his office. One day we mustered a mob of steers into the yards, including a couple of big grey bulls. Mal dusted off his bull-riding rope, greased up his riding glove and showed us the proper way of roping your hand down onto the back of the steer and we all took turns at falling off. It was definitely not pretty, but it was bloody good fun.

Nobody rode anything for more than five seconds that day, and those that rode the two big bulls didn't get very far from the chute. This was a problem because to qualify at the rodeo we'd have to stay on for at least eight. Chris bravely gave it a go and got kicked in the leg as he ran for the rails, and Dave sat up for a thrilling three seconds as the rest of us whooped and yelled with glee. Jimmy was the most successful rider. He lasted for what seemed like two minutes. It looked like slow motion as he swung and dived and spun on the back of the eight hundred-kilo monster.

Even Big Mick was having a hard time with a couple of extra-crazy buck-jumpers. The horses bucked so hard that Ray suggested they should enter them into the Daly Water Rodeo to challenge all the riders against a thousand dollar purse, 'For anyone who could ride time on a Murranji Maniac.' The rodeo was to start the following Saturday. It was officially going to last three days, but for a wild bunch of Northern Territory ringers the event was going to be celebrated at full-tilt for more than a week. Once a year the little town of Daly Waters, official population fifteen, turned into something more like the wild west.

I packed my swag and a change of clothes into my ute and on the Friday afternoon drove the hundred and fifty kilometres up to Daly Waters with Dave. Chris and Mal and some of the others travelled up that evening and Big Mick and the rest drove up on the Saturday morning. Dave and I drove into the big parking area just before sunset to find a sea of utes and horse trucks spread out for miles in every direction and Akubras and Stetson hats walking around on the heads of big packs of noisy ringers. More than four thousand people had descended on the town with money in their pockets and one main thing on their minds — beer. The crowd at the Daly Water Hotel was ten deep at the bar for about ten days, and the publican told me on one rare quiet occasion that he made enough money in those two weeks to cover never selling another beer all year. But he did, lots of them.

I couldn't help but join in with the other utes doing circle-work in the dust. Then I parked away from all the action and Dave and I headed for the pub. That night we drank about twenty beers between us, tried to pick up half a dozen girls, played lots of pool and got into two fights. All of which we completely lost in a miserable fashion. The scorecard was not looking all that good, but maybe the next day we'd have more luck.

There were a lot of sore heads walking around Daly Waters next morning. The first events were going to start at ten thirty and everyone started moving towards the center of all the action. The rodeo grounds were really just two big yards and a loading race up the middle with big steel swing gates for 'bucking out' the bulls and horses. The team-roping and other events were held in the yard over the back. A couple of shade structures with truck tarps as roofs acted as temporary beer tents, and there were forty-four gallon drums scattered everywhere for empty beer cans and rubbish.

All the ringers and jackaroos and jillaroos and tourists leaned through the rails to watch the action, or sat up on top like long lines of noisy galahs. The bulls came blasting out into the main yard with a rider hanging on as if his life depended on it, and often it did. There were two rodeo clowns walking around the ring helping 'faze' the bulls now and then by distracting the angry animals away from prone riders, and generally acting like idiots. The rodeo organisers didn't bother pushing the bulls out of the bucking yard each time a rider fell, they simply bucked the next animal and rider out and looked after the earlier ones later. At any time there could be six or seven angry bulls running around the rodeo grounds as riders were falling off.

This meant that you didn't only have to worry about the bull you were riding turning around and trying to kill you after you hit the ground, but you had the other contenders to deal with as well. Every now and then a couple of 'bull-catchers' were driven into the yard and all the remaining animals were pushed out. Bull-catchers are modified Tojos with no roof and no doors but solid bars all around and a big mechanical arm on the front, used to clamp down on a bull's neck as it was driven up beside the beast.

Like a kid watching a circus I didn't know which way to look first. Every time a bull was bucked out the crowd hushed for a short second, then we yelled and 'coo-eed!' in thunderous applause until the rider was thrown, and we'd gasp. Every now and then one of the loose bulls with its nostrils flaring ran at the rails and at the men and women perched up on top. People and hats and beer cans flew over the back and everyone roared with laughter as they hit the ground. The team-roping and barrel-racing events in the other yard were exciting to watch as animals and riders worked in harmony at a desperate task. Riders were leaning way out of their saddles as they threw ropes at speeding steers, and the horses kicked up dust as they galloped and then skidded to a stop.

Then it was Big Mick's turn on a bull. All the Murranji ringers were watching as he lowered himself onto the back of an angry-looking beast that was moving awkwardly back and forth in the bucking chute. Big Mick punched down on his riding glove with his other hand to lock it in as tightly as he could, then he pushed his big hat down hard on his head and yelled, 'Righto!'

The gate swung open and the rider and bull bucked out into the yard with all of us yelling our lungs out. The beast was huge. It had a large black hump on its shoulders that rippled with muscle as it bucked. Its two long thick pointy horns stood straight out to the side then curved upwards in a menacing arc. It pivoted around on its front legs as it spun and bucked. It was like bull ballet. Big Mick threw his left arm back and forth in rhythm. He gripped with his feet into the bull's flanks on the way down and straightened them out past its shoulders on the way up. The bull spun and bucked and shook its head and the crowd was screaming. It was the best ride of the day and eight seconds seemed like eight minutes before the siren went off.

Big Mick had planned in that split second to let go, jump off and run away from the steaming bastard that was thrashing around under him, but his hand was stuck tight. He fell to one side with his hand still wedged in his rope on the back of the bull and for about five seconds the big man looked like a rag doll as he hung off the side of the bull as it spun. His feet touched the ground every so often but there was nothing he could do to dislodge his hand and his arm was being stretched to breaking point. Luckily the clowns jumped in and fazed the beast. One of them ran straight at its head and leapt up and over as if in a game of leapfrog. This distracted the bull long enough to stop spinning while the other clown raced in and jumped onto its back and got Mick's hand to come free. They all ran for the rails as the angry animal ran at them with one last effort to kill and maim, and the crowd went crazy again. Big Mick came third that day. We told him he was ripped off.

Later that afternoon I lined up with the other ringers from Murranji and Newcastle Waters to have a go at staying on a steer. Back at Murranji I'd been practicing roping my hand down and checking my style with Big Mick and Mal as we practiced on an old forty four gallon drum suspended between two trees. But this was different. This was a living, breathing, thinking animal. The steer that was brought in for me when it was my turn was a thick, dark-grey animal. It seemed quiet enough as it stood in the bucking race and waited for me to adjust my rope and glove.

Then the gate swung open and suddenly the beast doubled in size and grew muscles that could propel it ten feet in the air. I lasted three ugly seconds before somersaulting over the steer's tail and hitting the ground on my bum.

Mal said very diplomatically that it was the most 'gymnastic' display of the day but Dave remarked that he'd seen children fall off bicycle's better. Mal and Chris got an honourable mention in the team-roping event and the others got their own pats on the back.

The Murranji ringers all had another go at riding steers the next day but we didn't impress anyone with our 'style.' If there was an event for yelling like a girl and throwing your arms around like a pelican while face-planting into the dust, then we would've taken home blue ribbons and gold trophies. As it was we had a bucket-load of beer each, and a lot of laughs. Rob gave us Monday off and said to be back at Murranji ready for work on Tuesday. 'No worries boss,' we all chimed in as we ran for the bar.

That afternoon as we were sitting around one of the tables out the front of the Daly Waters Hotel, a tourist bus pulled up and forty-two Japanese tourists piled out and started snapping away with the numerous cameras hanging around their necks. Two couples walked up and asked if they could get their photos taken with some 'real Australian cowboys.' A group of us happily obliged, hamming it up for the cameras. One of the tourists asked Mal if he could show him how to use the old skockwhip sitting on the table. Mal grabbed the little Japanese fellow around the shoulders with a friendly hug as he marched him out into the middle of the road. On the way he grabbed a packet of taylor-made cigarettes out of the pocket of one of the tourists and handed one to his new Japanese friend. People started gathering around in a loose circle.

The other Japanese tourists snapped away at their travelling companion while the blond Australian cowboy who was standing there swinging his stockwhip around his head motioned to the little bloke to hold the cigarette straight out in front and told him to, 'Stand very still.' The poor bloke was not sure, but he held the cigarette as directed. Everyone was silent. Except for the sound of camera shutters all you could hear was the 'woosh' of Mal's stockwhip. Then 'Crack!' The fella didn't even flinch as the cigarette went flying. The crowd noisily showed their appreciation as Mal walked up to the tourist and offered the pack of cigarettes to him once more.

He quietly motioned for him to put one in his mouth and made out like he was standing at attention. Mal didn't have to explain, it was pretty obvious, and scary, but great. His friends looked on approvingly as he put the cigarette confidently between his teeth and closed his eyes. Mal bent the man forward a little at his shoulders then walked back a few paces as he started swinging his stockwhip once more. Another loud 'Crack!' and the cigarette was gone. There was loud yelling and much clapping as Mal hugged his new best friend, and they walked back to the bar to have a beer together and laugh about what nearly just happened. As the Japanese fella walked alongside Mal he quietly checked his nose with his forefinger and thumb. I could tell he was relieved as he took a big gulp of his first Daly Waters ale.

Just then a horse walked into the bar. Straight through the front door, past our table and up to the bar, with its stirrups swinging sideways as it walked. The publican looked along the bar as the horse slowly licked ice from the beer taps and stuck its nose in the nearest schooner glass. 'I've told you a hundred times Cricket, you're not allowed in here with no money,' the publican said and the Japanese tourists went crazy. They thought it was the best thing that they'd ever seen. The mechanic at the nearby Kalala station was the owner of the horse and he spent the next hour giving the tourists rides on his beer-slurping stockhorse while they bought him drinks and took photos of anything that moved.

I found Dave around lunchtime the next day. He had cuts and bruises on his face and mud on his shirt. I asked him if he'd been bashing someone's fists with his face again as we had a couple of strong black coffees and then drove back to Murranji that afternoon.

'...at times we long to gallop where the reckless bushman rides, in the wake of startled brumbies that are flying for their hides. Long to feel the saddle tremble once again between our knees, and to hear the stockwhips rattle just like rifles in the trees! Long to feel the bridle-leather tugging strongly in the hand, and to feel once more a little like a native of the land.'

The City Bushman,
Henry Lawson 1892

CHAPTER 17
A Little Fishing

The bruises were nearly healed on Dave's face when Rob came over to the workmen's quarters after dinner one evening, to organise jobs and talk to Ray about his horse. He'd noticed that Shotgun had gone off his feed and was more lethargic than usual. They talked about mucus and manure, and sticking thermometers in dark places, and Ray suggested a good worming might help. Rob told Mitch and Chris they should organise the crate off the horse truck and drive to Newcastle Waters to pick up a tractor. They were going to have another go at laying the poly pipe to the horse trough in the front paddock that had gone so horribly wrong earlier in the season.

The other ringers were going to be mustering a mob out at Mud Bore and moving them back to the main yards. The buyers were coming in a week and the cattle had to be closer to the homestead. Rob told them he'd be down to draft the ugly ones off and then they'd let the rest go over in the 'Meadows' paddock behind the airstrip. Then he told me to pack my gear because in the morning Paddy the fencing contractor and I were going to drive to Daly River to pick up a couple of ponies for the kids.

Rob's two boys were continuously going somewhere with big grins on their faces and mischief on their minds. They liked killing snakes. They carried long twisted lengths of eight-gauge fencing wire which they used with deadly accuracy. I often rode past them as they walked up the airstrip with a couple of dead reptiles draped over sticks. Other times I'd see them running around the dam throwing rocks at diver-ducks, and then at each other.

The station kids had School of the Air for their reading and writing, and Murranji for everything else. They learnt bush skills and horse sense before they were ten years old. They recognised the changing of the seasons by the movement of birds and animals, and they knew how to pull an engine apart and how to drive a tractor before they turned twelve. They were really looking forward to having their own stockhorses so they could 'Muster with the big fellas like proper ringers.'

Dave said then that he was leaving. He asked Rob to make up his pay and if he could get a lift to Katherine with Paddy and me on our trip to Daly River. Rob said, 'No worries,' and walked back to the big house to write him a cheque. The next morning Paddy arrived early and we hooked up the horse float to the back of one of the station Tojos, grabbed Dave and left at about six o'clock. It was a quiet drive down to the Stuart Highway. All three of us sat in silence, enjoying the trip. I've noticed that men always seem content when they have somewhere to go, something to do.

As we left the dirt and turned left onto the highway, Paddy pushed an old Slim Dusty cassette into the truck's stereo. The sound was now very familiar. Most nights in the kitchen the ringers would play country-and-western on the stereo that sat on the fridge. However, when I had the kitchen to myself I'd turn the radio on, find a scratchy station and listen to the latest songs on the charts. It was a big year for Billy Idol with 'Mony Mony,' and Los Lobos with 'La Bamba.' I'd cringe when George Michael came on with 'I want your sex,' but live through it until U2 or Fleetwood Mac would come blasting through the little dusty speakers.

We drove straight through Dunmarra and on up the Stuart as the morning started to heat up. One hundred kilometres later we pulled up at Larrimah to fill up and stretch our legs. The Larrimah Hotel is well known up there for being completely relocated from its original place eight kilometres to the north, at the site of a large US Second World War airstrip. It also has the tallest bar in the country — the original bar had been extended thirteen inches during the war because the publican at the time had grown tired of drunken Americans jumping the bar and trying to pour their own beers. Things changed drastically for the flyboys the next time they went to the pub to blow off steam — they found the barman was suddenly thirteen inches taller (he'd raised the floor behind the bar as well) and the bar harder to hurdle. The publican's baseball bat was also closer to hand so things were a lot quieter from then on, at least inside the pub.

Dave and I were chatting about our experiences over the season at Murranji as we drove through Mataranka where the Stuart Highway turns northwest. We'd just about exhausted all our tall stories as we drove into Katherine around lunchtime. We filled up, grabbed some lunch, dropped Dave at the pub and said goodbye.

Paddy and I continued on, passing caravans, Tojos and road trains as we drove through Edith and up to Pine Creek. In one of Paddy's more talkative moments he told me the story of how Pine Creek had come to be. He was there in '78 and had plans to go back one day and drive those big loaders working twenty-four hours a day at the huge Pine Creek open-cut gold mine. 'Those boys earn about a grand a week,' he said. He was going to work half a year and then take the other half off and go fishing.

He explained that in the late 1800s a working party on the Overland Telegraph Line discovered gold at Pine Creek. The legend goes that a worker kicked a nugget the size of a football with his shoe as he walked along the telegraph track. That started Australia's biggest ever gold rush and so many people came to Pine Creek over the next few years they needed to divert the track to Darwin around the instant town sprang up.

We turned onto the Daly River Road and drove past the turnoff to 'Tipperary.' Paddy said that the Tipperary they were passing was a huge Northern Territory cattle station famous for its exotic animal zoo, not the subject of the old Irish ballad. Around four o'clock in the afternoon we pulled up outside a little fibro house on the edge of the Daly River and were instantly accosted by one of the biggest dogs that I'd ever seen. I recognised the head of a Great Dane but the rest of it looked more like a rhinoceros. It licked me on the elbow, and it needed to bend down to do it. Paddy said, 'Don't worry about him, it looks like he likes you. Good thing hey?'

As we moved towards the front gate of the garden I looked at a menagerie of animals. Two donkeys, a peacock on the porch, cockatoos in cages, a couple of goats and a camel in the side paddock reaching far over the low fence into the garden to nibble on a patch of purple and blue flowers. As we walked up the path to the porch we passed a fiberglass canoe with one end missing. A rough-looking bloke in a white singlet strode out onto the porch and said, 'A five metre saltie did that. Luckily I was close to the bank and I was able to get away.'

Paddy introduced the man to me as his cousin 'Reg' and we shook hands. Reg launched into a long explanation about the dangerous critters that lived around Daly River, about his numerous close encounters with saltwater crocodiles when he was fishing for barramundi, and about big angry wild water buffalo and packs of feral pigs that came through his vegies. He spoke of spiders that could kill you, venomous snakes that chased you, and a type of bat that chewed its way through your swag and bit your nose off. 'Losing your nose isn't really a problem compared to the horrible skin-wasting disease that the bat's saliva can give you,' he said. 'You want to come inside for a brew?'

'Yes please,' I said. I thought Daly River indoors was a much safer place than the Daly River outdoors right then. The 'brew' that Reg offered was not the billy tea I assumed, but a big thick glass of Reg's famous bitter ale homebrew. Paddy drank a proper cup of tea as I accepted a 'brew' from Reg, it tasted as though at some point it must have been a little like beer but then passed through the gut of a water buffalo before being left in the hot sun for a month. I tried to hide the screwed up expression on my face as I asked Reg about the camel outside. 'Well,' Reg replied, 'That old bastard's pretty harmless but he can spit twenty-feet. And he's deadly accurate.' Then he said to Paddy that we should go and catch dinner before it got too late. It was agreed that we'd catch a fish, cook dinner, have four or five more brews and look at the ponies in the morning.

Half an hour later I was perched up the front of a small dinghy being quietly pushed along a stretch of river by a silent electric outboard motor, with two men holding fishing rods out the back. Reg said to me, 'Keep a sharp eye out young fella,' and I wondered what the hell I was supposed to be keeping a sharp eye out for. Was it crocs or fish, or rocks or floating logs in the water that could wreck the little electric outboard motor? I didn't know, so I kept both eyes peeled for simply everything. The sky was growing darker and I definitely didn't want to be drifting down the river in the middle of the night with no way of getting back.

As we travelled along Reg quietly explained the art of finding, catching, cleaning and cooking barramundi. He said all barra' were born as boys and five years later they turned themselves into girls. One year of a barra's life was the same as five years of a human's so they 'made the change' at twenty-five years old. He said, 'I met a girl like that at a buck's party in Darwin once,' and laughed with a level of enthusiasm that rocked the little boat.

In the fish world, barramundi were like crocs, Reg said. They hang around in the shallows near rocks and old logs where they wait for unsuspecting meals to come by, 'They're smart buggers,' he said, 'You never know when they're gonna strike.' I hoped I wasn't going to end up an unsuspecting meal as I scanned the surface of the water for the nostrils of an approaching scaly monster. Paddy was sitting quietly in the back just watching his line as it trailed out behind when 'fzzzzzzz...' his reel started spinning and a big silver blur jumped out of the water about thirty metres from the boat. Paddy fought the rod and Reg yelled advice. The big barra jumped and bucked out of the water as it slowly came closer under Paddy's steady hands. Reg grabbed it in the net and held it aloft with glee. I could tell he'd done that move a thousand times before, and that he still enjoyed it every time. We turned the boat around and headed back to the jetty, to Reg's place for barra and brews.

Next morning we consumed a huge breakfast of bacon and eggs. I wondered if the bacon was from some wild razorback pig that Reg had just knifed and the eggs from a mother crocodile, but I wasn't game to ask. After breakfast we drove down to the horse yards to pick up the ponies. They were tiny black horses, not more than three feet tall, and they were quiet, soft and cute. Perfect for the Murranji kids. We loaded them into the horse float, packed bales of hay in the front and tied their miniature halters to the rail.

Paddy and I thanked Reg for his hospitality, his brews and his stories, and started the long drive back to Murranji. Reg promised he'd catch us a proper big barra the next time we came to visit. I couldn't believe that the huge fish we caught the evening before was not the biggest in the river. As we drove away I thought Daly River wouldn't be a bad place to live — if you didn't mind living in close proximity to dangerous animals that were constantly trying to hurt you. Then again, you get them everywhere.

CHAPTER 18

LEAVING TIME

I spent most of October tailing cattle and fixing fences, servicing the equipment and generally doing things that outback ringers do. I worked the horses, planted trees and tended the garden at the big house, and when there was nothing else on I drove into town for mail and supplies. On October 20th I was driving the old blue Tojo out to Buchanan with a forty-four gallon drum of diesel on the back, a rollie in my teeth and a grin on my face. At the same time the rest of the world was experiencing the single biggest stock market drop in history. The Australian All Ordinaries fell twenty-five percentage points in one day, commentators talked about a global recession and people were jumping off buildings on Wall Street. I didn't know, and even if I had I probably couldn't have cared less.

In nine months I'd not seen a lot of cash. I was provided lodgings and all the meat and damper I could eat. My wages of one hundred and twenty dollars a week (minus ten bucks for grog) were going to be calculated on the day I left and paid to me by cheque. I'd asked for some cash for one trip to town earlier in the season, and some more to spend at the Daly Waters Rodeo the month before, but other than that I had no need for money. The world economy was about as important to me as a box full of feather dusters, handy for somebody no doubt, just not me.

Big Mick drove away from Murranji towards the end of October, yelling at the others that they should 'learn how to ride properly before they came back next year,' and I took Chris and Mungo to meet the bus to Alice Springs not long after. Chris was going to go to Adelaide to spend some money on a girl he planned to meet and fall in love with, and Mungo had decided that the Alice might be a good place to spend Christmas, eating pudding and cake and Christmas turkeys. I wondered if it was a slip of the tongue or if he actually did mean whole turkeys. When I got back to Murranji I spent a night camping out at the blackfella's camp down below the homestead dam. I sat around the fire with Jimmy, Peter and Walter with his guitar. Walter showed me how to play Slim Dusty tunes and I showed him a couple of blues riffs I'd picked up down south. The next day I drove them all to the camp at Elliott and said a serious goodbye. I wanted to tell them that I was sad it was over, to say thanks for being friends, for watching my back and for helping me understand. Helping me to love the bush and appreciate the country. However, I didn't have to explain all that. They knew.

Mitch left a couple of days later and he took Mal with him. Before they left they ate a long lazy breakfast and even Rob didn't come down to wake anybody that morning. The rest of us just sat around and talked and smoked until late that morning. Mitch gave me his last piece of advice about the best way to pull a gearbox apart, and Mal told me to remember to 'ride lightly on the bit.' As he walked to Mitch's truck and jumped in he said with a big cheesy grin, 'You have to stay relaxed and don't tense up like you city boys are prone to do.'

Ray and I were left standing in front of the workmen's quarters as Mitch and Mal turned the corner around the workshop and went out of sight. 'So when do we leave,' asked Ray, and I paused before answering. 'Do we have to?' Ray said that Murranji was a real quiet place in the wet season. The track to town became really boggy and difficult to navigate so you simply stocked up with supplies and settled in for a couple of hot rainy months at the homestead. You got a visit from a chopper once or twice with the mail but you mostly just hung around the quarters and tried not to get bored. 'Have you got lots of reading to catch up on?' he asked me. 'Anyway, I need a lift to town,' he said as he walked back to his room and started packing his things.

Murranji Manager Robert Hale (left) and ringer Andy Hughes (right) saddled up and about to go mustering on Murranji cattle station, Northern Territory, 1987.

I looked at my old ute as I walked across the compound towards Rob's house. I thought I saw one of the headlights wink at me as if saying, 'Come on, let's go.' It must have been a reflection of the sunlight or some other trick of light. I talked to Rob about leaving. I had a long way to go and the wet season was coming. Then I was taken aback as Rob asked, 'Why don't you stay on? It's a long way to drive back from Sydney for the next trapping season.' I wanted to stay more than anything right then, to settle in for the wet and be part of it all for a whole other season. But I knew I had to go. Rob asked me to follow him into the office where he signed me a cheque, shook my hand and wished me good luck as he went back to his desk and a ringing telephone.

I said goodbye to Rob's family and for the last time walked back out the little iron gate at the end of the path to the Murranji homestead. Within the hour Ray and I had packed and were driving out past the workshop, the main yards and the horses in the front paddock. Ray placed a leather bag he was holding on the bench seat between us. 'This is for you,' he said simply, and went back to staring out the passenger side window at the horses, the fences and the track ahead. When I got to Elliott I left Ray at the pub and went to say farewell to Mary and Ron. I'd grown close to the storeowners over the course of the season and I was going to miss them very much. Ron cashed my cheque and then accepted some back for another pair of boots, a couple of fancy shirts and a new pair of jeans.

Mary actually gave me a hug, and Ron told me to take care. 'The city is never going to be the same place for you ever again young fella,' he said as he shook my hand and went back inside. As I drove away I thought how much the fancy shirt would make me look like the Darwin cowboys Mary complained about, but I could see her waving in my rear view mirror for a long time before she turned and followed Ron through the door.

I headed north with three thousand dollars burning a hole in my pocket. There were Darwin publicans who needed that money and I was keen to oblige. I opened the old leather bag Ray had put on the seat and tipped the contents out. It was Ray's good farrier's hammer, his carved hoof knife and pick. There was an old tin of number 4 nails, a pair of nippers and his old rasp. I marveled at the precious gifts. Ray had spent time showing me how to clean and trim hooves properly, how to use a shoeing hammer and how to fit a shoe. Long hours down in the horse yards practicing over and over with Ray saying things like, 'You've gotta' look after your tools,' and 'A farrier is no farrier without a decent shoe-hammer.' I gripped the wheel hard and sang along with the radio at the top of my lungs.

I stopped for petrol and food at Katherine and Pine Creek, had a drink at the Humpty Doo Hotel and then headed for Darwin. I'd joked with Mal before I left that when I finished the season at Murranji I was going to, 'Drive to Darwin, blow all my money, and then drive straight back to Sydney to start all over again from scratch.' Mal told me that the only place to stay if I was serious about this plan was the Darwin Casino — the MGM Grand.

I was dreaming of a hot bath when I pulled up in the Casino car park. I rolled seven hundred dollars up in an old sock and stuffed it under the springs of the bench seat for petrol and food on the long drive home. I grabbed my duffle bag, tobacco tin and wallet and walked up to the reception counter. The man behind the counter was clean and pretty in his shiny blue suit. He looked me up and down as he lifted my dirt-stained hand off the register book, apparently worried I might smudge it. I bought a room for four nights, a laundry service for everything in my bag, and breakfast in my room every morning. I caught the surprised look on the man's face when I paid for the whole lot, up front, with fifty-dollar notes.

I lazed around Darwin for five days. Every morning after a big breakfast I went for a swim, took a shower and walked through town. I bought new clothes, visited the East Point Military Museum and on The Esplanade and Smith Street ate lunch somewhere different every day. I did the tourist thing — I bought postcards and read books about the history of the city. Like most things in the Top End, Darwin was a resilient town. The Japanese tried to destroy it during the Second World War with bombs killing 243 people, and on Christmas Day 1974 Mother Nature had a go at trying to blow the city away, flattening three quarters of Darwin's buildings and killing 71 people.

I thought about my favourite Hoodoo Gurus song as I walked the streets — 'Tojo never made it to Darwin' — and I wondered if I'd ever get back to the Tojo at Murranji — the thirsty old blue truck. I thought about the many times I'd driven it to the Elliott Store, the many hours sitting under a shady tree waiting for the bloody thing to cool down. In my mind I was still there. I wanted to go back there, to rewind to March and play it all again, 'Now she's gone, gone, gone, just like the wind, I just sigh, I just sigh.'

At the Victoria Hotel I regaled fellow drinkers about big times at Murranji Cattle Station that year. I met old drovers, tourists and blackfellas, and they all had their own stories about their adventures across the Top End. Darwin still felt like a frontier, a rough town at the edge of the world. I spent a hundred dollars on bourbon at the Top End Hotel on the second night and won twice that back on the blackjack tables at the Casino on the third. I walked along Casaurina Beach and met a local who told me all about the deadly box jellyfish in the water, the deadly snakes in the mangroves and the deadly 'salties' up the other end of the beach. That kind of story didn't faze me anymore.

On my last night in Darwin I lost the last of my money on alcohol and blackjack, and crawled into bed as the sun was coming up. After a late breakfast I went down to the ute. I was planning to take a drive out to Fannie Bay before I checked out, but that was not to be. Someone had ripped open the tarp on the back and taken almost everything that I had of value. My swag, my old camp oven, toolbox, camping gear and esky. I was really going home with nothing more than I'd started with, but then again I had everything I wanted, a big life. I went back inside, packed my things, threw the room keys to the bloke behind the counter, and said, 'See you next trip' as I walked out the front door into the rain.

Over the next three and a half days I drove nearly four thousand kilometres. I got into a routine of driving for three and sleeping for one. I filled up at Katherine, Three Ways and at Camooweal — just across the Queensland border. Turning south at Cloncurry I travelled through Longreach, Roma and Goondiwindi. I felt light when I crossed over into New South Wales and went through Moree and Narrabri. It didn't matter if it was day or night, I just kept going.

Then south of Gunnedah I saw cars stopped in the middle of the road up ahead. I drove up slowly. There was a large mob of black cattle grazing along both sides of the road. Pulling up behind the last car I got out to check what was happening. Up front there was a Land Rover, a couple of stockmen, and a fallen cow. Blood was oozing from its nostrils and pooling on the bitumen, and I could see it was breathing heavily. There was a bloke standing in front of the Land Rover with one hand on his hip and the other scratching his head nervously.

I heard him say as I walked up, 'It ran straight out in front of me. What are we going to do now?' The stockmen's horses were tied up to the fence on the side of the road quietly munching on the tall, soft, grass. I noticed they were saddled long with breastplates and head-checks. Stockwhips were slung over the pommels of the saddles and each had a lariat tied to the back of the seat. One of the drovers said, 'She's done. Broken her shoulder and bleeding internally. We're gonna have to go back, get the truck, shoot her and drag her away.'

I knew what to do. I said, 'I'll look after it,' and went back to my ute. I drove around the others and pulled up in front of the cow on the road. I grabbed my towrope out of the back (one of the few things not pinched back in Darwin) and dropped it on the ground near the drover's feet. I ran the bench seat of my ute forward and pulled out the old .22 that was wrapped in a dusty saddle blanket. The other travelers drove around us and the man driving the Land Rover apologised as he got back in his vehicle and followed the others south. I cocked the rifle and looked at the older one of the two stockmen with the question on my face. 'Go ahead,' the bloke said, and I fired.

I shot true, just in the right spot, that imaginary 'x' spot that I'd drawn with my eye so many times before that year.

We hooked up the beast to the ute and I dragged it through a gate in the fence a hundred metres down the road. The two riders came up to me as I was coming back out onto the road after leaving the dead cow in the paddock behind a tree. I heard the familiar click of a loose shoe on the younger bloke's horse as I walked up. The older stockman said, 'Thanks, we'll take it from here old mate.'

'No worries,' I replied, 'But what about that loose jogger?' and I turned back to the front seat of the ute again. As I picked up Ray's old leather bag I thought to myself for the hundredth time since I'd left Darwin, 'Thank bloody hell those bastards didn't pinch my shoeing gear.'

Through Singleton, Newcastle and down the expressway to Sydney, the traffic got busier and the lights brighter. I sped down the Pacific Highway and turned south towards the house where I'd grown up. The tight little streets and the crowds of people, the cars and the flashing lights were as I remembered. But it all seemed unfamiliar and strange — it was a shock to come home. As long as I could remember I'd wanted to go bush, and I'd finally done it. It had taken all year to become a ringer, a stockman of the Northern Territory. A season full of lessons and transformations, but it had happened slowly, it had crept up on me.

Pulling up at the top of the driveway I could see mum and the others moving around in the front room with the light of the television flickering on the curtains. Looking down the steep driveway where I'd raced my brother in wooden billy carts to the spot where I'd fallen off my first bike, I could see the lights of Sydney in the distance over the roof of the house. This was where I'd spent my childhood, but somewhere else was where I'd spend the next stage of my life.

I looked up into the branches of the gum tree that I'd played in as a kid, the tree now towered over me as I got out and leaned on the open door of the ute. I felt the breeze and heard it rustle the leaves of the tree. 'Yep,' I thought happily as I started planning my next trip. 'South this time,' and I patted the roof with my hand.

A realisation hit me. I held my hands in front of my face, turned them slowly around, and smiled as I realised why the horse-breakers, the boss, and the storeowners were able to judge my credentials so quickly those early days at Murranji. My knuckles were now rough and I had short scars from many arguments with barbwire. My hands were lined and tanned, and they seemed stronger — they had character. It was easy to tell they no longer belonged to a 'city boy' at all.

Looking back the images are fading and the sounds are growing distant, but the adventure and the spirit is still kicking strong. I've told the story to friends and family, the tales have become bigger and the descriptions more vivid, but the wonder remains. The first time I roped a calf, drove a road train, or rode a steer. The first orange moon rise I witnessed from a swag in an outback stock camp on the edge of the desert. Nights that were so still I could lie in my swag under a cloudless sky and listen to my own heart beating. The harshness of the country, the boiling days and the cold nights. Chilly mornings riding out to muster another big mob, with the grass crackling under the footfall of the horses and cattle. Images that resembled a surreal movie set, something otherworldly, a wonder and beauty that changed me forever. Experiences that follow me through. Yes, it's tough country, and harsh on the unprepared, but I'd recommend it to anyone.

The End

Epilogue

Murranji today:

Through the 1990's, Aboriginal campaigners Pharlap Dixon and George King pursued a native title claim over a number of parcels of land in the Murranji and Newcastle Waters region. A successful claim was accomplished in September 2007 (FCA 1498).

After a period of decline and neglect the current owners of Murranji Cattle Station are busy rebuilding the property to be a working enterprise once again.

The Kimberley Killer:

Throughout 1987 roadblocks were set up across the northwest region of the Northern Territory, but the killer eluded the police dragnet and escaped across the border with Western Australia. Later in the year a helicopter pilot spotted a camouflaged vehicle in bushland near Fitzroy Crossing, and a team of heavily armed police from the elite Tactical Response Group in Perth was rapidly deployed to the area.

As the police approached an armed man, naked to the waist, he began firing. Officers dived for cover in the low-lying scrub and the order was given to open fire on the gunman. He was wounded, but continued to fire at police with his semi-automatic weapon. In the end the gunman was no match for the police team and he was soon found, killed by a bullet wound to the chest.

Police later identified the gunman as German tourist, Joseph Schwab, but to this day his motive for his random killings remains a mystery.